Buying Real Estate Foreclosures

Second Edition

Melissa S. Kollen-Rice

McGraw-Hill

New York   Chicago   San Francisco   Lisbon   London   Madrid
Mexico City   Milan   New Delhi   San Juan   Seoul
Singapore   Sydney   Toronto

1 2 3 4 5 6 7 8 9 0   AGM/AGM   0 9 8 7 6 5 4 3

ISBN 0-07-141238-7

This publication is designed to provide accurate and authoritative information in regard to the subject matter covered. It is sold with the understanding that the publisher is not engaged in rendering legal, accounting or other professional service. If legal or other expert assistance is required, the services of a competent professional person should be sought.
> —*from the declaration of principles jointly adopted by a committee of the American Bar Association and a committee of publishers*

 This book is printed on recycled, acid-free paper containing a minimum of 50% recycled, de-inked fiber.

Library of Congress Cataloging-in-Publication Data

Kollen, Melissa S.
    Buying real estate foreclosures / by Melissa S. Kollen-Rice.—2nd ed.
        p.   cm.
    ISBN 0-07-141238-7 (alk. paper)
    1. Real estate investment.   2. Foreclosure.   I. Title.
    HD1382.5.K65 2003
    332.63'24—dc21

                                                    2003007912

For Steve—My Best Friend, My Inspiration, My Knight in Shining Armor, and the Love of My Life
and
For Jimmy—My Pride and Joy, My Rising Superstar, and the Wealth of My Life
and
For Mom—My "Momager," My Heart and Soul, the Wind Beneath My Wings, and the Angel in My Life
and
For Tom and Maggie—My Guiding Lights of Love, Support, Wisdom and Kindness, and the Glow in My Life

Contents

List of Sample Forms, Illustrations, and Checklists   xi
Acknowledgements   xv
Introduction   xxi

1. Understanding Foreclosures   1

An Overview of the Legal Procedure   3
Mortgages and Deeds of Trust   5
   A Mortgage Foreclosure   8
   A Trust Deed Foreclosure   9
The Soldier's and Sailor's Civil Relief Act of 1940   10
Three Opportunities for Purchasing Foreclosures   10

2. The Basics of Buying Foreclosures at the Auction   13

A Day at the Auction   15
   Three Types of Auctions   15
   The Opening Bid Amount   16
   The Bidding Procedure   16
   The High Bidder   17
   Thirty Days to Close in Bank Auctions   17
   Unusual Closing Delays   17
Warning: Peculiar Purchase Ahead   21
   Buying for Less Than Market Value   21
   No Down Payment Refunds   21
   The Burden of Dispossessing Occupants   22
   Buying in "As-Is" Condition   22

The Delinquent Borrower's Right of Redemption   22
Unanticipated Liens You May Be Responsible for in Addition to the
    Purchase Price   23
Finding Upcoming Foreclosure Auctions   25
Foreclosure Auction List Publications   25
Announcements in Local Newspapers   27

3. The Basics of Buying Foreclosures after the Auction— From Banks   29

Defining Bank-Owned Properties   31
The Property Was Not Sold at the Public Auction   31
The Deed to the Property Was Returned to the Lender
    (a.k.a., a "Friendly" Foreclosure)   32
Redefining Bank-Owned Properties   32
A Lender's View of Bank-Owned Property   33
An REO Purchase Versus a Bank Auction Purchase   35
Finding REOs   36
Lending Institutions   36
Web Sites   36
Real Estate Offices   38
Word of Mouth/Observation   38
Preparing Your Offer   38
Negotiating Strategies That Help You Cut Through the Red Tape   40
Justify Low Offers with Documentation   40
Rise Above Your Competition   41

4. The Basics of Buying Foreclosures after the Auction— From Federal, State, and Local Government Agencies   43

Defining Government-Owned Property   45
Government Services Administration (GSA) Sales   45
Department of Housing and Urban Development (HUD) Sales
    (a.k.a. FHA Foreclosures)   46
Veterans Administration (VA) Sales   48
Federal Deposit Insurance Corporation (FDIC) Sales   48
Federal Home Loan Mortgage Corporation (Freddie Mac) Sales   49
Federal National Mortgage Association (Fannie Mae) Sales   49

5. The Basics of Buying Foreclosures before the Auction   51

Understanding the Delinquent Owners   53
How You Can Help   54
Negotiating with the Delinquent Owners—When the Property
    Has Equity   55
Negotiating with the Delinquent Owners—When There Is Negative
    Equity (a.k.a. "Short Sales")   56

Finding "Pre-Auction" Foreclosures   57
  Legal Notices In Local Newspapers   58
  Lis Pendens Lists   58
  Local Real Estate Offices   58
Contacting Delinquent Owners   58
  Once Is Not Enough   59
  Dress for Success   59
  Letters that Open Doors   59
  Envelopes that Beg To Be Opened   59
Additional Strategies and Tips for Buying Pre-Auction Foreclosures   61
  Include These Contract Terms   61
  Use the "B" (as in Bankruptcy) Word In "Self-Defense" if the Lender
  Is Unreasonable   61

6. Financing Foreclosures with Traditional Mortgage Loans   63

The Burden of Proof   65
Decisions, Decisions   65
Types of Mortgage Loans   67
  Conventional Fixed-Rate Mortgages   67
  FHA/VA Loans   68
  Balloon Loans   70
  Adjustable-Rate Mortgages (ARMs)   71
  Graduated-Payment Mortgages   71
Comparison Shopping for the Best Lender   71
Key Questions to Ask a Lender   72
For Fixed- and Adjustable-Rate Loans, Ask the Following Questions   72
For Adjustable-Rate Loans (ARMs), Ask the Following Questions   75

7. Creative Alternatives for Financing Foreclosures   79

Category #1: Foreclosure Purchasers with Limited Cash and
  Good Credit   81
  Put the Equity in Your Home to Good Use   81
  Obtain Financing from Banks and Government Agencies to Purchase
    (REO) Foreclosures from Their Inventories   83
  Obtain Financing from a Foreclosing Lender Before a Property
    Is Auctioned   83
  Get Your Foot in the Door with a Hard-Money Loan   84
  Build Wealth through Contract Transfers   84
  Borrow Against Whole Life Insurance Policies (Are You Sitting on
    Hidden Treasure?)   85
Category #2: Foreclosure Purchasers with Limited Cash and
  Tarnished Credit   86
  Buy Foreclosures with Partners   86
Category #3: Foreclosure Purchasers with a Lot of Cash and
  Good Credit   87
  All of the above Plus   90
  Buy Foreclosures with Cash at the Auction   90

Buy Foreclosures in Bulk from Banks and Government Agencies   90
Category #4: Foreclosure Purchasers with a Lot of Cash and
  Tarnished Credit   91
Purchase Now and Finance Later   91

8. Equity Sharing: Buying Foreclosures with a Partner   93

How It Works   95
Why It Works   95
The Owner-Occupant's Goals and Challenges   96
The Investor's Goals and Challenges   96
Owner-Occupants versus Investors—Comparing Purchases   98
Equity Sharing to the Rescue   101
Contract Terms to Agree Upon   102
The Risks Involved in Equity Sharing   108
Equity Sharing for Parents and Children   109
Equity Sharing for an Investor and a Contractor   109
Finding a Partner for Equity Sharing   112
Equity Sharing Helps People Achieve Their Goals   113

**9. Choosing the Right Property: What You Don't Know
   Can Hurt You   115**

Finding the Right Price   117
  Prequalified Versus Preapproved   117
  Questions to Ask a Lender when Shopping for a Preapproval   118
Finding the Right Property   119
  Getting Access   119
  The Preliminary Inspection   119
  Life-Saving Safety Tips for Inspections   120
  Once Is Not Enough   121
Asking the Right Questions   122
  Questions to Ask the Foreclosing Lender's Attorney, Referee,
    Real Estate Broker, Property Manager, or Other Designated Official   122
  Questions to Ask the Town/City Hall (Where the Foreclosure
    Is Located)   126
  Questions to Ask the Utility Companies (That Service the Premises)   130
Organizing Yourself   131
Inspecting the File of the Foreclosure Action   131
Hiring a Title Expert   131
Asking for the Terms of Sale before Bidding on Foreclosures
  at Auctions   131
Uncovering Hidden Costs   133
  A Homeowner's Insurance Policy   133
  Missing Property Documents   134
  Outstanding Utility Expenses   135

Repair Costs   135
Eviction Costs   135
Unpaid Property Taxes   135
Establishing Property Values   137
Calculating Cash Flow   138

10. Preparing Your Bid Sheet   **141**

Identify the Property's Condition   143
Condition 1: Vacant and Accessible   143
Condition 2: Occupied and Accessible   147
Condition 3: Vacant and Inaccessible   149
Condition 4: Occupied and Inaccessible   149
Final Confirmation   151

11. Congratulations! You Are the Successful High Bidder   **153**

When You Are the High Bidder at the Auction   155
When Your Offer for a Bank or Government-Owned Foreclosure
  Is Accepted   156
When Your Offer to the Delinquent Owner Is Accepted   156
Coast to the Closing with These Five Standard Operating Procedures   157
Standard Operating Procedure 1: Order Your Appropriate Insurance   157
Standard Operating Procedure 2: Protect the Premises   157
Standard Operating Procedure 3: Hire a Neighbor   158
Standard Operating Procedure 4: Order a Title Search and
  Title Insurance   158
Standard Operating Procedure 5: Apply for Your Financing
  (If Applicable)   159
Applying the Five Standard Operating Procedures to Your
  Particular Circumstances   160
After Contract: Implementing the Standard Operating Procedures for
  Vacant and Accessible Foreclosures   160
After Contract: Implementing the Standard Operating Procedures for
  Occupied and Accessible Foreclosures   160
After Contract: Implementing the Standard Operating Procedures for
  Vacant and Inaccessible Foreclosures   161
After Contract: Implementing the Standard Operating Procedures for
  Occupied and Inaccessible Properties   161
An After-Contract Checklist   163

12. Now That You Own the Property   **167**

Steps to Take for Completing the Transaction   169
Record the Closing Documents   169
Schedule the Repair Work   169
Restore the Utility Services   169

Begin Eviction Proceedings (if Applicable)   170
Contact Your Local Tax Collector   170
Execute the Lease   172
After-Closing Checklist   172

13. Making Repairs to Your Foreclosure   173

Pinpointing Priorities   175
Finding a Contractor   175
Implementing a Competitive Bidding System   176
   Conducting the Initial Interview   176
   Preparing the Bid Package for Estimates   177
      The Specifications   177
      The Notice to Bidders   188
      The Bid Summary Sheet   191
   Setting Up a Comparative Cost Analysis Worksheet   192
   Awarding the Job   192
Implementing a Performance-Based Payment Plan   195
   Establishing an Escrow Account   196
   Developing the Contractor's Agreement   196
   Other Contract Terms to Include   197
The Big Picture   201

14. Getting Started Today   203

Follow These Six Steps for Success in Purchasing Foreclosures   205
   Step 1: Arrange Your Financing   205
   Step 2: Develop Your Network of Support   206
   Step 3: Send for Your Foreclosure Lists   206
   Step 4: Review Your Foreclosure Facts   207
   Step 5: Select the Property That Is Right for You and Do a
      Trial Run   207
   Step 6: Don't Give Up   207
From Rags to Riches with Real Estate Foreclosures   209

Index   211

List of Sample Forms, Illustrations, and Checklists

Chapter 1

Figure 1-1. An Example of a Mortgage Loan Default   4

Figure 1-2. A Sample Deed of Trust   6

Figure 1-3. A Sample Note and Mortgage   7

Chapter 2

Figure 2-1. A Standard Deed   18

Figure 2-2. A Torrens Title   19

Figure 2-3. A Bank Auction Purchase Versus a Traditional Purchase   26

Figure 2-4. A Sample Legal Notice From a Newspaper   28

Chapter 3

Figure 3-1. A Bank Auction Purchase Versus an REO Purchase   37

Figure 3-2. An Example of an Offer Letter for a Bank-Owned Property   39

Chapter 4

Figure 4-1. An Illustration of a HUD Advertisement   47

Chapter 5

Figure 5-1. An Example of a Letter to a Delinquent Owner   60

Chapter 6

Figure 6-1. A Comparison Between a 15-Year and a 30-Year Mortgage after 5 Years   69

Figure 6-2. A Sample Spreadsheet for Comparing Mortgage Programs Offered By Lending Institutions   72

Chapter 7

Figure 7-1. Refinancing a 10-Year-Old Mortgage   82

Figure 7-2. Taking Out an Equity Loan or a Second Mortgage   82

Figure 7-3. A Contract Transfer   85

Figure 7-4. A Sample Partnership Arrangement   88

Figure 7-5. A Sample Partnership Arrangement—Three Equal Partners   89

Chapter 8

Figure 8-1. Owner-Occupant versus Investor—Comparing Purchases   99

Figure 8-2. A 90-Percent/10-Percent Split Under an Equity-Sharing Arrangement   103

Figure 8-3. An Equity-Sharing Arrangement between Parents and Their Child   110

Figure 8.4. An Equity Sharing Arrangement Between Contractor and Investor   111

Chapter 9

Figure 9-1. A Certificate of Occupancy   127

Figure 9-2. A Survey   128

Figure 9-3. A Sample Checklist of Prebid Questions   132

Figure 9-4. A Sample Engineer's Report   136

Figure 9-5. An Example of a Cash Flow Projection for a Single-Family Dwelling   139

Chapter 10

Figure 10-1. Bid-Calculating Worksheet   145

Figure 10-2. Sample Checklist: Prior to Bidding   150

Chapter 11

Figure 11-1. An Example of a "Greetings" Letter to Cooperative Occupants   162

Figure 11-2. An Example of a "Greetings" Letter to Uncooperative Occupants   164

Figure 11-3. Sample Checklist: After the Contract   165

Chapter 12

Figure 12-1. Sample Checklist: After the Closing   171

Chapter 13

Figure 13-1. Bid Specification Worksheet—Exterior Work   179

Figure 13-2. Bid Specification Worksheet—Kitchen   180

Figure 13-3. Bid Specification Worksheet—Bedroom   181

Figure 13-4. Bid Specification Worksheet—Bathroom   182

Figure 13-5. Bid Specification Worksheet—Living Room   183

Figure 13-6. Bid Specification Worksheet—Dining Room   184

Figure 13-7. Bid Specification Worksheet— Hallway   185

Figure 13-8. Bid Specification Worksheet—Plumbing/ Heating/Electrical Work   186

Figure 13-9. Bid Specification Worksheet— Miscellaneous   187

Figure 13-10. Bid Specification Worksheet Completed by Owner—Exterior   189

Figure 13-11. A Notice-to-Bidders Form   190

Figure 13-12. A Bid Summary Sheet   193

Figure 13-13. Comparative Cost Analysis Worksheet   194

Figure 13-14. A Sample Contractor's Agreement   198

Figure 13-15. A Sample Contractor's Extension Form   200

Chapter 14

Figure 14-1. "Getting Started Today" Checklist   208

Acknowledgments

Buying Real Estate Foreclosures: Revision, 2003

When McGraw-Hill requested this revision, I was trying to juggle the demands of a full-time job (daytimes), running my real estate school classes and performing my seminars on weekends, and attending law school four evenings a week. My schedule was already quite challenging—okay, *insane*—and I wasn't sure that I could find any more hours to squeeze out of each day. There is no question, therefore, that this project could not have been accomplished without *unwavering* support, cooperation, and encouragement from my family, my friends, my co-workers at PM Realty Group, and my "mentors" at Touro Law School. I gratefully acknowledge the following people for their invaluable contributions to this updated edition:

My Family

To **Steve,** for being the sanity and the sanctity in my life, for loving me so flawlessly, and for treating me "like a diamond" every day of my life. Your unselfish support, sacrifice, and faith in me are the foundation of my happiness, and your love is the driving force behind everything I accomplish.

To **Jimmy** for having the courage and drive to achieve excellence–thank you for understanding and supporting my dream and for being the best son any parent could hope for. From the moment you were born, it has been, is, and will always be my privilege to be your mother.

To **Mom**, for being my manager, my lifelong role model, and my brave angel. Thank you for bringing me up in an environment that values advocacy and compassion.

To **Jack**, for letting me "adopt" you and for being such an honorable, beloved addition to our family.

To **Tom** and **Maggie**; your love and support are proof that you don't have to be blood-related to be "family."

To **Matt** and **Beth,** and **Lindsey** and **Kim**, **Laura** and **Bob, Sharlene, George,** and **Sharlet** for being so patient and supportive in arranging holidays and birthdays around my crazy schedule. and for forgiving my absences so graciously.

My Literary Support System

Mary Glenn, my editor, for being on my team and guiding this book through to production.

Olga Weiser, my literary agent; as always, thank you for making this happen.

My Media and Professional Support System

Daria and **Ken Dolan** *(Smart Money, CNBC Radio and Television)* for being such gracious, warm and compassionate hosts, for your dedication to enhancing the quality of life for your viewers and listeners.

Joe Catalano *(Newsday Staffwriter/Contributor)* for your support, your words of wisdom, and your commitment to helping others improve their lives.

Kevin Woods *(Owner of FSBO and Foreclosure World)* for sponsoring my Foreclosure Seminars, and for many, many years of friendship and support.

Bill Davis *(Owner of the LI Profiles)* for your dedication to your subscribers, and your kindness in providing me with the tools to help foreclosure purchasers in their quest for success.

Cathy Nolan, Atty, for your friendship, brilliant legal insights, upbeat sense of humor, and for being such an inspiring mentor.

My PM Realty Family

F. Mark Hagendorf, for my "I love NY" excursion, bolstering my self-confidence, honing my "corporate" skills, and for providing me with the support I needed to meet any new challenge. I will cherish your glorious spirit, your meticulous sense of style, and your outrageous antics for the rest of my life.

Robert C. Midgette, for your friendship, your leadership, for your faith in me professionally, and for "guiltlessly" allowing me the flexibility to meet a grueling schedule. I could not have done all of this without you.

Ed Keaveny, for taking a chance on me, and for teaching me that a winning team is rooted in a spirit of mutual respect, loyalty, quiet dignity, encouragement, and cooperation.

Geri Guccione, for the sunshine, wisdom, and love you bring me, and for being such an incredible source of positive encouragement to me every day.

Fran Spilkevitz, for your "can do" approach to getting the job done, for being our "office mommy," and for saving me from "rubber bands."

My **PM Realty Group** co-workers and "partners" in Brooklyn, on Long Island, in New Jersey, in Delaware, and in Houston. I have never met a more professional, hard working, talented, loyal group of "winners." In the words of our esteemed leader, Jimmy Gunn, "There are no 'I's in our 'team.'" I am *so proud* and so honored to be associated with the people in this company.

My Touro Law School Family

I want to gratefully acknowledge **Dean Glickstein**, my professors, the staff, and the faculty at Touro Law School, Huntington, New York, for helping me attain my lifelong dream. A few words of special mention are extended to the following people who have had a profound effect on my law school experience, as well as my ability to think, write, and reason. They are presented in alphabetical order:

Professor Ilene Cooper, for introducing me to the world of trusts and estates, for being so helpful and kind and for having enough energy to power a small country!

Professor Suzanne Darrow Kleinhaus, for taking me under your wing and guiding me through the "essay" maze, and never letting me get discouraged.

Professor Jonathan Ezor—for your inspiring introduction to the "wild west" of cyberspace. I am now a huge fan.

Professor Louise Harmon, for contributing your valuable feedback on property matters, and for sharing your brilliant, humorous insights on life.

Professor Brannon Heath, for setting high standards of excellence and giving us the tools we needed to reach that level, for helping me when I had problems "muddling through," and especially because "everything they say about you *is* true."

Professor Eileen Kaufman, for bringing our Constitution and it's "creators" alive with your unparalleled ability to make words flow like a melody, and for always having a positive, kind, and supportive word when I need it the most.

Judge Lazer, for showing me how to prepare opening and closing statements that *do not* put a judge to sleep, and for your outstanding sense of humor.

Dean Nicole Lee, for taking the time to meet with me, advise me, and offer words of wisdom when Touro was just a dream in the horizon, and for continuing that tradition of availability from the day I became a student at Touro.

Beth Mobley, for showing me the nuts and bolts of legal research in a law library, and for making it such a positive learning experience.

Professor Jeffrey Morris, for introducing us to criminals we will never forget, and for always letting us know how much you care.

Judge Pratt, for introducing me to the Federal Rules, Lucy Lockett, and my first Federal Court trial.

Dean Kenneth A. Rosenblum, for organizing my life and comforting me when the "crazies" set in, and for always making me feel like I am exactly where I am supposed to be.

Professor Gary Shaw, for challenging me to keep pushing myself beyond my comfort zone, for investing so much time in helping me to improve, and for your "stand-up comedy" lectures that had us rolling in the aisles.

Professor Ted Silver, for making the UCC so clear, for your wit, sense of humor, and unforgettable illustrations—and because everyone *does* need "something nice" once in a while.

Professor Howard Stein, for providing me with the legal context I needed to complement my real estate experience. Thank you for solving so many mysteries!

Susan Thompson, for giving me my first impression of Touro, my acceptance letter, (and great directions to the ladies room!). You are the reason I never considered going anywhere else.

Professor Peter Zablotsky, for your unforgettable rendition of "Boston Edison," your Bush-Gore play-by-play during the 2000 presidential elections that kept us on the cutting edge of the controversy, and for your friendship, compassion, and efforts on behalf of my mom.

Acknowledgment Excerpts from *Buying Real Estate Foreclosures,* First Edition, 1991

I would like to gratefully acknowledge the following people for supporting this project with unlimited contributions of their time, advice, and expertise:

David Conti, my publisher at McGraw-Hill, whose belief in me and my ideas has turned a lifelong dream into reality.

Olga Wieser, my agent at Wieser & Wieser, for her encouragement and kindness.

W. Adam Mandelbaum, attorney, for sharing his legal expertise.

Tom Caulfield (Suffolk County Title Insurance Co.) for contributing so much of his time and support and for sharing his expertise on the intricate aspects of title work.

Walter Eidelkind (Long Island Realty Co.) for providing the setting for where it all began, the "golden keys" to unlock the doors, and the opportunity to use them to the best of my potential.

George Wexler, C.P.A., for his guidance and expertise relating to financial and investing matters.

Joanne Von Zwehl (RDA Enterprises) for her enduring support, ongoing encouragement, and many contributions from an investor's viewpoint

The following people have helped me tremendously with their expertise in financing and their insights into a lender's view of bank-owned foreclosures:

Robert DiBella, Green Point Savings Bank.

William Holihan, Citibank, NA.

Ray Ludwig, Long Island Savings Bank.

Eleanor Cutlar, The Dime Savings Bank.

Tom Riccobono, Norstar Bank.

Katherine Spears, information specialist, Resolution Trust Corporation.

John Reno, Reno & Arturo, Esq. for his expert counsel and advice on landlord-tenant legal matters.

Martin John Yate, author, for the gift of his friendship and for easing my path through the doors of the literary world.

Taucher-Chronacher, Professional Engineers, P.C., for invaluable assistance in the art of building inspections and for allowing me to use portions of their forms for illustrative purposes in this book.

Introduction

How many of you have bosses who stay up late at night thinking of ways to help *you* make a lot of money? On the other hand, how many of you have worked diligently for others, for many years, and have made *them* a lot of money? You will never get ahead by waiting for a boss to give you what *you* think you deserve. You have to take control of your own destiny.

Whether you are a renter who is in pursuit of the "American dream of home ownership," or an investor who is looking to build wealth, *Buying Real Estate Foreclosures* will help you to achieve your goal, *safely* and *sanely*. By choosing real estate in general, and foreclosures in particular as your vehicle to success, you have joined thousands of entrepreneurs who started out along the same path as you are now—with a dream and the motivation to attain it.

The vast majority of people use their money to buy furniture, furs, jewelry, and other luxury items. But in five years, will a $5000 living room set be worth more, or less? The answer, of course, is *less*. Entrepreneurs are different. We want more. We will forego immediate gratification for future gain, and we look to buy things like real estate, which will be worth *more* in five years.

Now, I am not going to tell you that buying foreclosures is a "get-rich-quick" endeavor. With few exceptions, everything that is rewarding in life requires some investment of our time and effort. But the ratio of the effort expended in relation to the success that is generated makes purchasing foreclosures incredibly worthwhile.

Who Would Be Interested in This Book?

This book is designed especially for the following types of readers nationwide, regardless of experience level, occupation, or financial status:

Renters who wish to purchase a home at an affordable price.

Investors who wish to purchase properties at below-market prices and either fix them up and "flip" them (i.e., sell them) for a quick profit, or keep them and rent them out to tenants while the properties build up equity.

Real estate professionals who wish to help customers and clients buy foreclosures, help delinquent owners sell their homes to prevent foreclosure, and/or to help locate sources of bank and government listings to sell to their customers and clients.

Contractors who wish to buy a foreclosure that needs work, complete the repairs at a minimal cost, and then sell it for a profit, or keep it to live in.

Entrepreneurs who wish to build wealth by buying and selling foreclosures for a profit.

Accountants who wish to help their clients buy foreclosures as tax shelters.

Attorneys who want to help their clients purchase foreclosures, or to help their clients who are in danger of defaulting on their mortgage loans, to prevent foreclosures.

Parents who wish to learn creative techniques for purchasing real estate with their children.

Landlords who wish to buy foreclosures for use as rental property that yields monthly rental income and yearly income tax deductions.

The list is seemingly endless...

Why This Book Is Unique

I began an extensive career in real estate when I worked for a multifaceted firm that specialized in residential investing, mortgage brokering, and residential property management. At that time, there was a limited selection of books or courses available to help me get started. Therefore, with no previous experience in the real estate field, I was guided by common sense; an innate ability to react with immediacy and remedial action when faced with new challenges; trial and error; and the parameters set forth by my industrious, entrepreneurial employers. Thankfully, I didn't make a lot of mistakes—at least, not more than once!

With more than a decade of experience under my belt in buying, selling, renting, managing, and creatively financing hundreds of real estate properties, I wanted to make it easier for those who followed in my footsteps. *Buying Real Estate Foreclosures* was written as a hands-on guidebook that was based on my own real-life experiences. I have been in the trenches. I have had the same questions, doubts, and feelings of inadequacy that many people encounter when they try something new. I knew that providing easy-to-follow, step-by-step procedures for buying foreclosures could help motivate people who wanted to expand their horizons by instilling in them the confidence they needed to pursue their dreams.

Of course, there are other books on the market for people who wish to buy foreclosures, but this book is unique for three reasons. First, it prepares the reader to buy foreclosures using practical, street-smart techniques. Second, it explains potential roadblocks (such as unfriendly occupants and missing legal documents) and gives proven, practical methods for resolving these issues safely and sanely. Third, the book is geared to *all* levels of experience. Beginners as well as experienced foreclosure purchasers will appreciate the checklists that have been written for every phase of the foreclosure purchase in a logical, organized manner. Beginners will appreciate learning about potential problems they may face *before* they make costly mistakes, and experienced buyers will relate to the "war stories."

Finding What You Want

The topics in this book have been organized in the following manner:

Understanding foreclosures. The legal procedure behind a foreclosure action is explained to provide readers with an insight into how a lender forecloses on a delinquent borrower. Knowledge of the foreclosure process helps potential buyers identify optimum purchasing opportunities that arise at specific intervals throughout the procedure, recognize certain statutory regulations that may affect purchasing decisions, and begin a new venture with a strong foundation to build upon.

Buying foreclosures at the auction. A typical day at an auction is described, including the procedures for buying a foreclosure at an auction; what bidders are expected to do; what bidders *may not* do; and the step-by-step procedures for bidding on a property, from inspection through closing.

Buying foreclosures after the auction.   The opportunities to buy repossessed foreclosures from bank and government agencies are described and defined. Also uncovers why banks and government agencies are so highly motivated to sell these properties, and the step-by-step negotiating strategies that help you cut through the red tape and rise above your competition. Sources of bank and government agency foreclosure lists (telephone numbers and Web sites) are included to help you get started. Finally, to give readers more of a global prospective, buying foreclosures from a bank's inventory is contrasted with buying foreclosures at bank auctions.

Buying foreclosures before the auction.   The benefits and techniques for finding, approaching, and negotiating with delinquent homeowners before the lender forecloses are revealed and explained.

Financing foreclosures.   Readers are taken behind the scenes of a mortgage application and furnished with mortgage descriptions and checklists to help them compare the lenders and their loans. Creative strategies are detailed for buyers in four categories: those with limited cash and good credit, those with limited cash and tarnished credit, those with a lot of cash and good credit, and those with a lot of cash and tarnished credit. Partnership strategies and equity sharing options and agreements are also detailed.

Choosing the right property: what you don't know *can* hurt you.   Readers are introduced to the step-by-step procedures, homework, legwork, and research skills that play an essential role in selecting the right property to buy and in calculating the right price to pay.

Preparing your bid sheet.   The information that was gathered during the preliminary preparations is organized into one simple bidding form for all kinds of foreclosures to help readers prioritize their wants and needs, finalize their price ranges, and narrow down their selections to those that are most worth pursuing.

Steps to take when your offer is accepted.   The five standard operating procedures are explained for buyers when 1) they are the high bidders at auctions; 2) their offer for a bank or government foreclosure is accepted, and 3) they have successfully negotiated the price and terms for pre-auction foreclosures with delinquent owners. Also includes a checklist to help buyers prepare for the closing.

Steps to take after you own the property. Six after-closing tasks and a detailed checklist are provided to help readers complete their foreclosure purchase.

Making repairs to your foreclosure. Two techniques —a "competitive bidding system," and a "payment for performance" initiative—help readers select the right contractor, itemize their specifications, and negotiate the best price and payment terms. It includes sample cost-analysis worksheets, sample bid specifications, and a sample contractor's agreement.

Getting started today. Readers are given six simple steps to turn their dreams into reality today.

Other Major Features in This Book

1. Introductions to each chapter that define its purpose, its context within the overall foreclosure-purchasing process, and how it will help the reader.

2. Ten innovative methods for financing foreclosures for each reader's individual situation.

3. Twenty-two questions that will help you distinguish a "dream" from a "disaster."

4. Six hidden additional costs to expect when buying a foreclosure.

5. How to get free real estate property values.

6. How to approach angry, unfriendly occupants and get past "the guy with the pit bull and the shotgun."

7. Three lifesaving safety tips.

8. Six steps to take to turn your dreams into reality today.

9. Forty-eight usable sample forms, illustrations, and documents.

10. A bid-calculating worksheet for buying foreclosures safely and sanely, and avoiding "auction fever."

11. Sample form letters that compel a response from reclusive delinquent homeowners, and from cooperative and uncooperative occupants living in the foreclosed property that you want to buy.

12. Offer letters to send to banks for REOs in their inventories, and techniques for cutting through the red tape when you present your offer.

13. Checklists with procedures for bidding, steps to take after the contract, steps to take after the closing, questions for determining the true value of the property, and steps to take for getting started today.

14. Charts that compare and contrast the differences in purchasing strategies: a traditional purchase versus a bank-auction purchase; a bank-auction purchase versus an REO purchase; purchasing as an investor versus purchasing as an owner-occupant.

15. What the banks can't tell you about the REO properties in their inventories.

1

Understanding Foreclosures

Each state in the United States has its own legal procedures for taking foreclosure action. We can, however, find a common ground in the basic principles that trigger the commencement of foreclosure actions, and in the judicial guidelines that help navigate the actions as they travel through the state court systems. In Chapter 1, we introduce the legal procedure that occurs when a lender forecloses. Knowledge of the foreclosure process helps potential buyers: (1) identify optimum purchasing opportunities that arise at specific intervals throughout the procedure; (2) recognize certain statutory regulations that may affect purchasing decisions; and (3) begin a new venture with a strong foundation to build upon. In upcoming chapters, we bolster this foundation with proven techniques for buying foreclosures safely and sanely.

An Overview of the Legal Procedure

A foreclosure action is the legal procedure that a lender initiates to reclaim ownership and possession of a property after the borrower fails to repay the loan in accordance with the contractual terms. The foreclosure procedure terminates those rights that the borrower had secured, either through a mortgage or a deed of trust.

As an example, suppose we have a mortgage loan with terms that stipulate that the loan will be in default after the borrower, also known as the "delinquent homeowner,"* is 90 days late with the monthly loan payment (see Figure 1-1 for illustration).

In our example, the mortgage balance at the time of default is $90,000, and the borrower's monthly mortgage payment is $1000. After missing one monthly payment, the borrower is 30 days late, and owes the lender $1000 (plus late charges). After missing the second consecutive monthly payment, the borrower is 60 days late, and owes the lender $2000 (plus late charges). After the borrower misses the third consecutive monthly payment, the loan payment is 90 days late. Rather than owing the lender $3000 (plus late charges), at this point, in accordance with the 90-day default provision, the due date of the mortgage loan accelerates and the lender may call the entire remaining mortgage balance of $90,000 due and payable in full. If the borrower in our example is unable to pay

* In this book, the terms *"delinquent borrower"* and *"delinquent homeowner"* are used interchangeably because within this context they are synonymous.

3

Mortgage Loan Default

(When Loan Terms Allow Foreclosure as a Remedy after Monthly Loan Payments Are 90+ Days Late)

Mortgage Balance—$90,000

Monthly Payment—$ 1,000

❑ Miss 1 payment (30 days late)

Owe $1,000 *plus late charges*

❑ Miss 2nd consecutive payment (60 days late)

Owe $2,000 *plus late charges*

❑ Miss 3rd consecutive payment (90 days late)

Owe $90,000 *plus late charges*

❑ Loan period is accelerated

Entire outstanding balance of $90,000
plus late charges is due now.

Figure 1-1. An example of a mortgage loan default.

off the entire mortgage balance and cannot work out an alternative repayment plan with the lender, the lender may opt to sell the property at an auction in order to recapture its losses. The auction will be held at a designated location that is open to the public, such as the county court house, town hall, etc. The public is notified according to local custom, usually through advertisements published in the town, village, or city newspapers. A referee is appointed to accept verbal bids on behalf of the foreclosing lender from those who attend the auction, and will award the contract of sale to the highest bidder. The duration of the foreclosure procedure, from its initiation until its completion, is determined by whether the instrument that created the borrower's obligation to repay the loan was a mortgage or a deed of trust.

Mortgages and Deeds of Trust

Mortgages and deeds of trust are the legal instruments that create a lien against the borrower's property. On a nationwide scale, the states are about equally divided in their statutory adoption of mortgages and deeds of trust, and a few states even use both.*

The deed of trust and the mortgage serve virtually the same purpose; however, a major difference is found in the length of time it takes a lender to foreclose on a delinquent loan—approximately 12–18 months for a mortgage foreclosure compared to approximately 4–12 weeks for a trust deed foreclosure. The mortgage foreclosure process is longer in duration because it requires the foreclosing lender to initiate a judicial procedure through the court to obtain a judgment of foreclosure and sale. By contrast, a trust deed default triggers a strict foreclosure action that can be completed in a fraction of the time it takes to foreclose a mortgage because, under a deed of trust, title remains with the lender until the loan is paid in full; therefore, no lengthy court action is required for the lender to reclaim the right to sell the property when the loan is in default.

Figure 1-2 is an illustration of a deed of trust, and Figure 1-3 is an illustration of a note and mortgage.

The length of time it takes for a lender to foreclose can dramatically affect a foreclosure purchasing strategy. For example, a buyer who wishes to purchase a foreclosure in a trust deed state (where the foreclosure action is completed in a shorter time frame) would implement a more intense plan of action due to the abbreviated schedule for completing

* To learn more about the instrument that is used to secure a loan on real property in your state, you can contact your State Bar Association and ask for the names of attorneys in your area who specialize in real estate and/or foreclosure transactions. Title companies and lending institutions are also sources to contact for more information.

DEED OF TRUST

Date:

Grantor:

Grantor's Mailing Address (including county):

Beneficiary's Rights
    1.   Beneficiary may appoint in writing a substitute or successor trustee, succeeding to all rights and responsibilities of Trustee.
    2.   If the proceeds of the note are used to pay any debt secured by prior liens, Beneficiary is subrogated to all of the rights and liens of the holders of any debt so paid.
    3.   Beneficiary may apply any proceeds received under the insurance policy either to reduce the note or to repair or replace damaged or destroyed improvements covered by the policy.
    4.   If Grantor fails to perform any of Grantor's obligations, Beneficiary may perform those obligations and be reimbursed by Grantor on demand at the place where the note is payable for any sums so paid, including attorney's fees, plus interest on those sums from the dates of payment at the rate stated in the note for matured, unpaid amounts. The sum to be reimbursed shall be secured by this deed of trust.

Trustee's Duties
    If requested by Beneficiary to foreclose this lien, Trustee shall:
    1.   either personally or by agent give notice of the foreclosure sale as required by the Texas Property Code as then amended;
    2.   sell and convey all or part of the property to the highest bidder for cash with a general warranty binding Grantor, subject to prior liens and to other exceptions to conveyance and warranty; and
    3.   from the proceeds of the sale, pay, in this order:
        a. expenses of foreclosure, including a commission to Trustee of 5% of the bid;
        b. to Beneficiary, the full amount of principal, interest, attorney's fees, and other charges due and unpaid;
        c. any amounts required by law to be paid before payment to Grantor; and
        d. to Grantor, any balance.

FOR ILLUSTRATION PURPOSES ONLY. REPRODUCTION PROHIBITED.

Forms may be obtained through State Bar of Texas (512) 463-1463

Figure 1-2. A sample deed of trust.

CONSULT YOUR LAWYER BEFORE SIGNING THIS FORM–THIS FORM SHOULD BE USED BY LAWYERS ONLY.

NOTE AND MORTGAGE

$.................................   Date................................

Parties   Mortgagor

Mortgagee
Address

Promise to pay
principal
amount (debt)
interest
payments

Mortgagor promises to pay to Mortgagee or order the sum of

dollars ($)

with interest at the rate of   % per year from the date above until the debt is paid in full.
Mortgagor will pay the debt as follows:

Application of payments   The Mortgagee will apply each payment first to interest charges and then to repayment of the debt.

Address for payment   Payment shall be made at Mortgagee's address above or at any other address Mortgagee directs.

Transfer of rights in the Property   Additional promises and agreements of the Mortgagor:

1. The Mortgagor hereby mortgages to the Mortgagee the Property described in this Note and Mortgage. Mortgagor can lose the Property for failure to keep the promises in this Note and Mortgage.

Property Mortgaged   2. The Property mortgaged (the "Property") is All

Figure 1-3. A sample note and mortgage.

the transaction. On the other hand, a buyer who wishes to purchase a foreclosure in a mortgage state (where the foreclosure action takes longer) would have more time to implement a plan of action. In the next paragraphs, we look at the procedural differences in mortgage and trust deed foreclosures.

A Mortgage Foreclosure

In those states where a mortgage instrument has been adopted, when real property is mortgaged, the borrower signs two separate instruments: the note (or bond), which is evidence of the borrower's promise to pay the debt; and the mortgage, which is the legal instrument that creates the lien on the property as security for the debt. If the mortgagor, or borrower, fails to make payments, then the mortgagee, or lender, must take action to collect the amount due. Lenders have a policy in place for dealing with borrowers who fall behind on their loan payments. The lender usually sends a letter advising the borrower that the mortgage payment is late, and requesting the borrower to remit the payment immediately. If the payment remains in arrears, many lending institutions will continue their attempts to contact the delinquent borrower. The lender wants an explanation for the nonpayment, and an opportunity to work out a plan to bring the mortgage payments current. Is the delay temporary? Is the situation that caused the delinquency unusual and unlikely to reoccur? Will the delinquent borrower be able to resume making payments very shortly?

If the mortgage cannot be brought current, or if the delinquent borrower is unresponsive or uncooperative, the lending institution hires an attorney, who will begin a foreclosure action to protect the lender's interests. The attorney initiates the foreclosure action on behalf of the lender by ordering a *foreclosure search*. This is a report from a title company that provides the attorney with information about the property owner, the mortgagee, and other creditors who have an interest in the property. In this manner, the foreclosure search ascertains that the party named as the defendant in the foreclosure proceeding is, in fact, the legal property owner. Other creditors may include second mortgagees, mechanic's lien holders, judgment holders, utility companies, and federal and state income tax and property tax lien holders.

Next, the attorney files legal documents, including a *summons* (the notice directing the defendant to appear in court), *a complaint* (the plaintiff's allegations of entitlement to relief and the relief sought), and the *lis pendens* (the legal document that "gives notice to the world that there is a legal action pending on this property"). The documents are filed with the clerk of the court in the county where the property is located. Once the *lis pendens* is filed, any additional liens or judgments against the property may be excluded from the foreclosure action, and those creditors will have to initiate legal proceedings against the delinquent owner's assets independently.

After the attorney files the necessary documents with the court, all parties named in the action (including the delinquent borrower, the creditors, tenants of the owner, trustees, etc.) must be served with the legal notices. Each state has enacted statutes that regulate foreclosures, including the time periods within which legal documents must be filed. For example, some states require the delinquent borrower to be served within 30 days of the filing date of the *lis pendens*. Another example is where the delinquent borrower has a tenant residing in the property that the lender is foreclosing on. In that case, some states require the tenant to be named as a party to the action and served with notice, or the successful high bidder may have to honor the terms of the current lease that exists between the delinquent borrower and the tenant until the lease expires. If the mortgagor fails to respond to the complaint within the statutory time limit, the attorney submits a report to the court stating the facts of the case and requesting the court to appoint a referee. The referee reviews the facts and circumstances in the foreclosure action and renders his or her report to the court. The judge then issues a Judgment of Foreclosure and Sale in favor of the foreclosing lender.

The auction sale is advertised in accordance with local statutes. At the auction, the referee reads the *terms of sale* to the public and starts the bidding at the "upset price" (the dollar amount stipulated by the courts in the Judgment of Foreclosure and Sale).

A Trust Deed Foreclosure

Trust deeds are similar to mortgages except that the trust deed is a three-party instrument. The borrower is called the *trustor,* and the lender is the *beneficiary.* The third party is an intermediary, called the *trustee.* The trustee's job is to hold the title to the property on behalf of the beneficiary, as security for the payment of the debt. Due to the *power-of-sale* clause found in all trust deeds, if the trustor does not make the loan payments, the trustee can sell the property at a public auction without having to obtain permission from the courts. The trustee simply records a notice of default, sends a copy to the trustor, and after the statutory period, notice of sale is posted on the property.

The sale is advertised to the public for the required period of time, and if payment is still not made by the trustor to cover the arrears, the property is auctioned. Lenders prefer trust deeds to mortgages because they can auction the property and recapture their losses much faster. It is most important to remember that *lenders are not required by law to foreclose.* However, should they choose to do so, they must follow the procedure mandated by the laws of the state where the property is located.*

The Soldier's and Sailor's Civil Relief Act of 1940

In some cases, a lender must modify a foreclosure action in order to comply with the *Soldier's and Sailor's Civil Relief Act of 1940.* Under this act, when property is owned by a person who is in active military duty, and the mortgage loan was originated prior to the commencement of that military duty, then no sale, foreclosure, or seizure of property for nonpayment of any sum due will be valid if it is made during the period of the military service, or within several months thereafter. This does not apply if the courts think that the ability of the delinquent homeowner to comply with the terms of the loan obligation is not materially affected by the homeowner's involvement in military service, or if the foreclosure sale was granted by the courts before the active duty began. Under the act, active-duty military personnel may be allowed a reduction of interest rates on debts, including mortgages, if their military service involvement impairs their ability to pay their loans at the current interest rates. Repayment plans and extensions of time to pay can also be worked out. Consult a mortgage expert, your State Banking Department, and/or an attorney who specializes in foreclosure purchases and sales for more information about the specific foreclosure procedures that apply in your state.

Three Opportunities for Purchasing Foreclosures

Now that we know how a property finds its way to the foreclosure auction, in the chapters that follow, we will be covering the step-by-step procedures for purchasing foreclosures, and the benefits and risks associated with each of the three opportunities to buy foreclosures:

---

* Since both the deed of trust and the mortgage serve similar purposes, in order to simplify the text and avoid the need to discuss each instrument separately in each chapter, throughout this book, I will refer to "mortgages."

1. At the Auction (Chapter 2)

The borrowers have defaulted on the mortgage loan payments, and the lenders seek to recapture their losses by offering the properties for sale at public auctions.

2. After the Auction (Chapters 3 and 4)

Lending institutions and government agencies sell repossessed foreclosures to the public from their inventories.

3. Before the Auction (Chapter 5)

Delinquent borrowers, about to be foreclosed on, try to avoid losing their equity, their credit rating and even their future income by selling the property *before* the lender forecloses on it.

2

The Basics of Buying Foreclosures at the Auction

The first opportunity for purchasing foreclosures is found at foreclosure auctions. Foreclosure auctions are court-ordered sales whereby the lender of a mortgage in default seeks to recapture its losses by selling the property to the highest bidder at a public auction. In Chapter 2, we describe what to expect on a typical day at a foreclosure auction. Understanding the overall procedure will help buyers determine if foreclosure auctions are the best opportunity available for reaching their personal financial goals.

A Day at the Auction

To put this event into perspective, we are at a point in the foreclosure process where the borrower defaulted on the mortgage loan and the lender is seeking to recapture its losses by offering the property for sale to the public at an auction.

Three Types of Auctions

There are three kinds of auctions that sellers use to covey real and/or personal property. An *absolute auction* is a type of auction whereby the seller must accept the highest bid, no matter how low it is. This type of auction poses a risk to the seller, especially when the high bid is lower than the market value of the item, and is more suitable for events such as an auction of personal property at a charitable event.

The next type of auction, an *auction with reservation* is one where, in contrast with an absolute auction, the seller reserves the right to reject any offer from a bidder, no matter how lucrative that offer may be.

Finally, a *minimum bid auction* is one where the seller establishes a starting amount to begin the bidding. All bids must exceed that amount, and the highest bidder is awarded the contract. This is the type of auction that is used for mortgage foreclosures.

To begin a typical day at a mortgage foreclosure auction, let's review the overall "minimum bid" procedure.

The Opening Bid Amount

Before the foreclosure auction commences, the *opening bid amount,* also known as an *upset price,* has been established to begin the bidding. The opening bid amount usually includes the unpaid mortgage balance, interest and back taxes, court costs, legal fees, and the liens and judgments attached to the premises during the time that the delinquent party owned the property. These debts are normally satisfied at the closing with the money paid by the successful high bidder.

The Bidding Procedure

When I attended my first foreclosure sale, I had visions of an auctioneer wielding a huge gavel and *"yodeling"* bid amounts from behind an oversized podium. Instead, I was surprised to find that, after the referee announced that the sale was about to begin, verbal bidding was conducted in a quiet and organized manner—with no yodeling and no gavel!

Although many people attend auctions, not everyone is there to bid on a property. Some people go to auctions merely out of curiosity. Others go to familiarize themselves with the auction procedure before they bid, to reduce the "intimidation factor" that arises when people are about to embark on a new venture.

At some foreclosure auctions, you may find yourself in a bidding war with ten other people, in which case, the person with the highest offer will be awarded the contract for the purchase of the property. On the other hand, you may find that you are the only one attending the auction. Should this happen, you will be able to buy the property at the opening bid amount because there are no competitors there to "bid up" the price.

When the auction begins, the referee explains the bidding procedure to be followed, and identifies the property (or properties) up for bid. By "identify," I mean that the referee recites the legal description of the property and any related tax map designations. Details such as distinctive structural features that make the property more attractive to a buyer (i.e., professional landscaping, outdoor hot tub, in-ground pool, central air conditioning, etc.) *are not* mentioned because they are not considered relevant to the "legal description." Later, in Chapter 9, we will look at how to inspect a foreclosure before you purchase it. Ideally, the improvements to the property should be identified and evaluated as part of your pre-bid preparations —before you even decide to attend the auction.

Statutory provisions govern the procedures that are implemented for auctioning foreclosures. In some states, auctions are conducted through *verbal bidding,* in which the bidder *calls out* an offer for the property that he or she wishes to purchase. Another method used for bidding at auctions involves *sealed written offers*. The written offers are given to the designated authority, who opens them and announces the successful high bidder's name and bid amount. Some auction regulations require bidders to register before the auction, at which time they must provide proof that, if they are the high bidders, they have with them the financial resources necessary (usually 10 percent of the high bid) to pay the down payment. Attending the mortgage or trust deed auctions in your locality to familiarize yourself with the bidding process is an essential step in preparing to buy foreclosures at auctions, and is discussed in more detail in Chapter 14.

The High Bidder

The high bidder is usually awarded (the equivalent of) a contract of sale. If you, as high bidder, are awarded the contract, you will be expected to render a required down payment (usually 10 percent of the bid amount) immediately in the form of a money order, bank check, or certified funds, as required by the referee. (In Chapter 9, we review the people to contact to get the down payment information, and in Chapter 10 we cover how to calculate your 10 percent down payment.)

Thirty Days to Close in Bank Auctions

You will be expected to "close" with the 90-percent balance due within a certain period of time—usually 30 days after the contract is signed at the auction. Under certain circumstances, you may be granted an extension (extra time to close). For example, if your attorney is on vacation, you may need to ask for an extension until he or she returns. Normally, however, if you are the successful high bidder at a foreclosure auction, you will be expected to close within the 30-day period stipulated in the contract.

Unusual Closing Delays

I was once involved in an unusual circumstance in which the *referee*, appointed by the court to sell the property at the auction, required an extension of more than a year because a necessary legal document was missing. Before I explain the details of this case at greater length, some background information on the nature of the document in question is in order.

In many states, real property is conveyed either through a deed (see Figure 2-1) or a *Torrens title* (see Figure 2-2), also known as an "Owner's

CONSULT YOUR LAWYER BEFORE SIGNING THIS INSTRUMENT—THIS INSTRUMENT SHOULD BE USED BY LAWYERS ONLY.

THIS INDENTURE, made the   day of   , nineteen hundred and
BETWEEN

party of the first part, and

party of the second part,

WITNESSETH, that the party of the first part, in consideration of Ten Dollars and other valuable consideration paid by the party of the second part, does hereby grant and release unto the party of the second part, the heirs or successors and assigns of the party of the second part forever,

ALL that certain plot, piece or parcel of land, with the buildings and improvements thereon erected, situate, lying and being in the

TOGETHER with all right, title and interest, if any, of the party of the first part in and to any streets and roads abutting the above described premises to the center lines thereof; TOGETHER with the appurtenances and all the estate and rights of the party of the first part in and to said premises; TO HAVE AND TO HOLD the premises herein granted unto the party of the second part, the heirs or successors and assigns of the party of the second part forever.

AND the party of the first part covenants that the party of the first part has not done or suffered anything whereby the said premises have been encumbered in any way whatever, except as aforesaid.
AND the party of the first part, in compliance with Section 13 of the Lien Law, covenants that the party of the first part will receive the consideration for this conveyance and will hold the right to receive such consideration as a trust fund to be applied first for the purpose of paying the cost of the improvement and will apply the same first to the payment of the cost of the improvement before using any part of the total of the same for any other purpose.
The word "party" shall be construed as if it read "parties" whenever the sense of this indenture so requires.

IN WITNESS WHEREOF, the party of the first part has duly executed this deed the day and year first above written.

IN PRESENCE OF:

Figure 2-1. A standard deed.

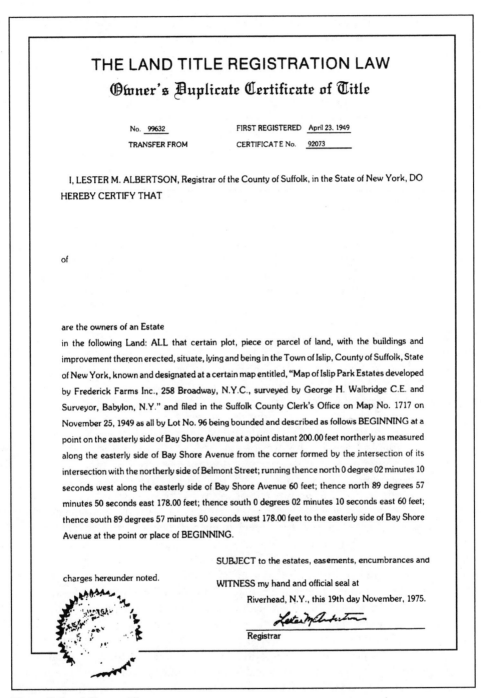

THE LAND TITLE REGISTRATION LAW
Owner's Duplicate Certificate of Title

No. __99632__   FIRST REGISTERED __April 23, 1949__

TRANSFER FROM   CERTIFICATE No. __92073__

I, LESTER M. ALBERTSON, Registrar of the County of Suffolk, in the State of New York, DO HEREBY CERTIFY THAT

of

are the owners of an Estate

in the following Land: ALL that certain plot, piece or parcel of land, with the buildings and improvement thereon erected, situate, lying and being in the Town of Islip, County of Suffolk, State of New York, known and designated at a certain map entitled, "Map of Islip Park Estates developed by Frederick Farms Inc., 258 Broadway, N.Y.C., surveyed by George H. Walbridge C.E. and Surveyor, Babylon, N.Y." and filed in the Suffolk County Clerk's Office on Map No. 1717 on November 25, 1949 as all by Lot No. 96 being bounded and described as follows BEGINNING at a point on the easterly side of Bay Shore Avenue at a point distant 200.00 feet northerly as measured along the easterly side of Bay Shore Avenue from the corner formed by the intersection of its intersection with the northerly side of Belmont Street; running thence north 0 degree 02 minutes 10 seconds west along the easterly side of Bay Shore Avenue 60 feet; thence north 89 degrees 57 minutes 50 seconds east 178.00 feet; thence south 0 degrees 02 minutes 10 seconds east 60 feet; thence south 89 degrees 57 minutes 50 seconds west 178.00 feet to the easterly side of Bay Shore Avenue at the point or place of BEGINNING.

SUBJECT to the estates, easements, encumbrances and

charges hereunder noted.   WITNESS my hand and official seal at

Riverhead, N.Y., this 19th day November, 1975.

_____
Registrar

Figure 2-2. A Torrens title.

Duplicate Certificate of Title" (ODC). Torrens titles originated many years ago in Australia as the method used in that country to record real property transactions. However, deeds and Torrens titles are *not* interchangeable documents. One cannot be replaced with the other.

An original Torrens title is manila-colored and has a gold seal on the front page. Also on the front page is a legal description of the property, just as in a deed. But, unlike a deed, the Torrens title contains a listing of the *memorials* that includes all the legal instruments (mortgages, liens, judgments, and satisfactions) that have been recorded on the property from its origins.

The deed or Torrens title, depending on which of the two is used, will be among the important documents sent to a new homeowner after it is recorded. From that point on, if a homeowner loses a deed, it can be replaced for a few dollars simply by requesting a duplicate copy from the office of the county clerk in the county where the property is located. If a homeowner loses a Torrens title, however, a *court order* is required in many states to replace it with another original Torrens title. This procedure can take many months, and as I mentioned, in one foreclosure purchase in which I was involved, it took well over a year! In states where the Torrens system has not been simplified, when property under a Torrens title is conveyed, the original document must be updated to reflect the details of the new transaction (i.e., the seller's mortgage loan satisfaction, the purchaser's name(s), new mortgagee information, etc.). Because the original Torrens title is most likely in the possession of the delinquent homeowner who is about to be foreclosed on, it is oftentimes difficult for the foreclosing lender to obtain the document. Predictably, the delinquent borrower is unwilling to cooperate with the foreclosing lender by making the document available because this would expedite the sale of the borrower's home to someone else. If the original document cannot be obtained, the foreclosing lender must go through the courts to get a replacement Torrens title in order to convey the property to the successful high bidder.

That being said, we can return now to the case with the missing documents. In that situation, the delay occurred because the foreclosing lender was unable to obtain the original Torrens title from the delinquent borrower. As a result, the successful high bidder (an investor for whom I was managing the property) had to wait more than a year until the referee was able to obtain a replacement for the original Torrens title through the courts. The investor ended up benefiting from the experience because he had plenty of time to secure financing and work out a rental agreement with the occupants. This is not to imply that the procedure to obtain a new Torrens title will *always* take as long as it did in this case. Your state may have legislation that makes it unnecessary for a lender without the original Torrens certificate to go through the courts for a new one. Contact your attorney or title expert for more information as to whether or not the Torrens system is operative in the areas where you wish to purchase foreclosures.

Warning: Peculiar Purchase Ahead

Foreclosure auction purchases are different from a traditional purchase between a buyer and a seller. Let's look at the distinguishing character- istics that make this type of transaction so unique.

Buying for Less Than Market Value

Normally, you pay close to market value, or maybe a little less, for a tra- ditional property purchase. For a foreclosure purchased at an auction, however, you could end up paying a *small fraction* of the price you would have paid for a traditional purchase, because the purchase price is based on the *mortgage balance* and *not* on the market value.

I know of an investor who purchased a property at an auction in Westhampton Beach on Long Island, New York that was worth approxi- mately $1 million . . . for $167,000! He was the only bidder at the auction and bought the foreclosure for one dollar over the upset price. The auc- tion just happened to take place on the day of a hurricane! While this is certainly an extreme example, many "seasoned" foreclosure purchasers vow that the best time to bid on a property is during poor weather con- ditions, when fewer people venture outside to attend an auction!

No Down Payment Refunds

In a traditional purchase, there is usually a *mortgage contingency clause* in the contract whereby, if you are unable to obtain financing from a lender to purchase the property, you are entitled to have your down payment refunded. However, when a foreclosure is purchased at an auction, there is *no* mortgage contingency clause allowing down payment refunds. If you cannot come up with the cash required to complete the transaction within the contractual 30-day period, you could *lose* your down payment.

Check with the referee, and/or have your attorney examine the contract to confirm that the down payment itself would be considered the total amount of "liquidated damages" and that you would not be held responsible for the difference between your original bid amount and the re-auctioned amount if the property were subsequently sold for less money.

A gentleman who attended one of my seminars on buying fore- closures told me that he was planning to participate in his first auction the following day. He intended to bring his family's life savings of $15,000 with him to use as his down payment if he was the successful high bidder. He didn't realize that the contract would require him to close within 30 days; he expected the referee to wait for him to get a mortgage in order to close—even if it took several months. He literally turned pale and broke out into a cold sweat when he learned how close he had come to losing everything!

The Burden of Dispossessing Occupants

In a traditional purchase, you can expect the premises to be "broom-clean" and vacant on the closing date, unless other arrangements have been made in advance between the buyer and the seller. When you buy a foreclosure at an auction, however, the burden of dispossessing any of the current occupants falls on the high bidder, after the closing has taken place.

Buying in "As-Is" Condition

Another distinction between properties purchased at foreclosure auctions and traditional purchases involves representations about the property's condition. In a traditional purchase, you expect the plumbing, heating, electrical systems, and appliances to be in good working order, and the roof to be free of leaks. Because foreclosure proceedings are indicative of a distressed situation, you cannot expect the same representations that the property is in good repair. Foreclosure purchases are sold in "as-is" condition. What you see, or don't see, is what you get—or don't get! People who are losing their homes are not likely to keep up with repairs or cosmetic appearances. You must remember that when buying a foreclosure, you are not dealing with a traditional seller whose contract terms usually require the property to be sold in good condition. Instead, you are dealing with an entity, the lending institution, and the referee's sole function is to sell the property at the highest price possible in order to mitigate the lender's losses.

The Delinquent Borrower's Right of Redemption

Another foreclosure auction idiosyncrasy is the delinquent homeowner's *right of redemption*. The right of redemption is available to everyone who owns real estate and, in the foreclosure auction context, it allows the delinquent homeowner to reclaim his property by rendering the entire outstanding debt (the upset price) up until the moment that the public auction begins.

In some states, the delinquent homeowner's right of redemption allows him to reclaim his property from the high bidder *even after* the auction by paying the upset price plus interest. In other states, the delinquent homeowner's right of redemption expires once the bidding begins, in which case the only way to reclaim the property is by being the successful high bidder. Check with your attorney to confirm the redemption procedures that apply in your state.

Unanticipated Liens You May Be Responsible for in Addition to the Purchase Price

In a traditional purchase, you can expect that the property you are purchasing has no outstanding liens, except for the financing you borrowed to purchase it. On the other hand, when you purchase a foreclosure at an auction, there may be unexpected liens you are responsible for, in addition to the purchase price.

For example, if the foreclosure action is on a first mortgage, no problem; the high bidder takes the premises free and clear of junior mortgages. The second (and third, etc.) mortgagees would have to recover the outstanding amounts due from the delinquent owner personally, by filing an independent action for a judgment against him and seizing other assets he may own in the county. (This is why second mortgages are so much more expensive than first mortgages—borrowers are really paying for the greater risk of loss that second mortgage holders incur.)

By contrast, if the foreclosure action is on a second mortgage, the high bidder takes the premises "subject to" the first mortgage, meaning that, in this case, the first mortgage is another expense that must be paid as part of the purchase. Prospective bidders who have "done their homework" are aware that they are bidding on a second mortgage. Some people work out an assumption of the first mortgage balance with the first mortgagee; others simply apply for enough new financing to cover the amount needed to pay off both the old first and second mortgages.

To illustrate these concepts, let's compare how you would be affected if you were bidding at an auction on a property where the <u>first mortgagee</u> was foreclosing, and another where the <u>second mortgagee</u> was foreclosing. In both situations let's assume that the market value of the property is $250,000, Also assume that there is a first mortgage balance in the amount of $100,000 and, a second mortgage balance in the amount of $50,000. Now, let's look at what happened when the property owner experienced financial difficulty and could only afford to pay one, but not both, of the two mortgages loans.

If the homeowner only paid the second mortgage, the first mortgagee is foreclosing. The upset price to begin the auction is $100,000 (the unpaid balance of the first mortgage) plus legal fees, etc. To simplify our illustration, let's say you are the only bidder at the auction (so no one bids up the price), and you are awarded the contract for $100,000 (plus legal fees, etc.). You take the property *free and clear* of the second mortgage. (As stated earlier, the second mortgagee has to recapture its losses by filing liens against other assets owned by the delinquent homeowner.) As the successful high bidder for this first mortgage foreclosure, you purchased a property valued at $250,000 for $100,000.

On the other hand, if the homeowner only paid the first mortgage, but could not afford to pay the second mortgage, the second mortgagee is foreclosing. The upset price is $50,000 (the unpaid balance of the second mortgage) plus legal fees, etc. Again, let's say you are the only bidder at the auction, and you are awarded the contract for $50,000 (plus legal fees, etc.). You are the new owner of the premises, *subject to* the first mortgage (of $100,000). You either negotiate with the first mortgagee to assume the balance of the loan in your name, and make monthly payments over a pre-agreed period of years, or, if the first mortgagee requires payment in full, you would have to apply for enough financing to cover your $50,000 high bid on the second mortgage, plus $100,000 to pay off the existing first mortgage. As the successful high bidder for this second mortgage foreclosure, you purchased a property valued at $250,000 for $150,000.

In cases where the high bid amount at the auction exceeds the upset price, the overage (a.k.a. "surplus") goes to pay off the second mortgage and other creditors (named as defendants). If there are no other mortgages or creditors, the surplus goes to the delinquent homeowner.

There are several ways for foreclosure purchasers to distinguish whether the foreclosure action is on a first or a second mortgage, depending on your experience level. The most foolproof method (and the one that I recommend for foreclosure purchasers who are not experienced title professionals) is to hire a title company to perform a "last owner search," also known as a "mortgage, lien and judgment search." Much less extensive (and <u>much</u> less costly) than a title search, the "last owner" search provides an accurate summary of the instruments that affect the property, and is the best way to ensure that you have the correct information about the position (first, second, third, etc.) of the mortgage you are bidding on. Going forward, if you are the high bidder, you will most likely want to order a full title report, but until you know that you are the high bidder, why go to the expense of a full report? Contact your attorney or a title company for more information about this type of search.

If you know your way around the county clerk's office, and are familiar with real property documents, you could search the public records to see whether more than one mortgage was recorded on the property that you are interested in. If there is more than one mortgage, the first one recorded is usually the first mortgage—except in cases where a subordination agreement was filed.

You can requisition the foreclosure file from the government office in the county where the action arose. Look for wording in the legal documents indicating that the foreclosure is on a "purchase money" mortgage. If so, the mortgage was given as security for the loan when the delinquent owner originally purchased the property (as opposed to a refinance or a second mortgage loan) and you will most likely be bidding on a first mortgage.

Figure 2-3 compares and contrasts the aforementioned characteristics that distinguish foreclosure auction purchases from traditional purchases.

Finding Upcoming Foreclosure Auctions

Foreclosure Auction List Publications

There are companies that publish lists of upcoming foreclosure auctions in the form of newspapers, magazines, newsletters, etc. The lists are also available to subscribers who wish to purchase them through the Internet.

The following questions can help you decide which foreclosure list provider offers the best services for the best price.

What information do they include in their publication? Obviously, the more information supplied to you, the subscriber, the better. Here are some of the features I have found to be most helpful:

- A picture of the property
- The number of rooms in the property
- The dimensions of the rooms
- The appraised value
- The lot size

A TRADITIONAL PROPERTY PURCHASE
VERSUS
A FORECLOSURE AUCTION PURCHASE

BUYING FROM A TRADITIONAL SELLER	BUYING AT A FORECLOSURE AUCTION
1. The asking price is based on market value	1. The asking price is based on the unpaid mortgage balance plus expenses.
2. The contract terms normally include a "mortgage contingency clause."	2. The contract terms do not include a "mortgage contingency clause."
3. The premises are conveyed in "broom clean" and vacant condition.	3. The burden of evicting the current occupants is on the new owner, after title is conveyed.
4. The plumbing, heating, electrical systems, and the appliances are in working order, and the roof is free of leaks.	4. The plumbing, heating, electrical systems, and the appliances and roof are sold in "as-is" condition.
5. The seller has no right of redemption after title is conveyed to the new owner.	5. The delinquent owner's right of redemption may extend beyond the auction date.
6. The seller usually clears up any existing title problems (i.e., liens and judgments) before title can be conveyed to the new owner.	6. The new owner may be responsible for unexpected liens and judgments on the premises, in addition to the purchase price.

Figure 2-3. A bank auction purchase vs. a traditional purchase.

- Whether or not the property is registered by deed or by Torrens title (if applicable)
- The property address
- Directions to the auction location
- Time, place, and date of the auction
- The current mortgage balance
- The name of the foreclosing lender
- The lender's attorney information (name, address, and telephone number)
- The referee information (name, address, and telephone number)
- The index number of the action

What states/counties/towns do they cover? If you are interested in properties that are located in more than one county or township, you would need to know whether they are all included in the publication. On the other hand, if you are only interested in one specific county or township, you may not need a publication that covers a much larger area.

How often does the publication come out? Foreclosure auction lists come out weekly, biweekly, and even monthly. My preference is for lists that come out weekly. The idea is to get the listings that give you the most lead time, before the auctions begin, to complete your prebid preparations.

Do the publishers offer support services and advice if you are a subscriber? This service can be extremely valuable for inexperienced foreclosure purchasers and might make the difference in your choice of one publication over another.

What is the publisher's fee, and do they offer discounted rates if you subscribe for longer periods? Some publishers will charge you a lower price if you subscribe to their publication for a longer term (that is, for six months rather than three months, or for one year rather than six months, and so forth). Also, ask whether the fee is discounted if you subscribe to more than one county or township.

Announcements in Local Newspapers

Pursuant to state laws, a foreclosing lender may be required to publicize the upcoming auction. You may be able to find this information in the legal notices section of your local newspaper. Figure 2-4 is an illustration of a sample legal notice. The legal notice usually includes the name of the foreclosing lender, the delinquent homeowner(s), the index number purchased when the action was filed, the legal description of the property, and other information required by the laws of the state.

```
L-8704
SUPREME COURT—COUNTY OF

       SAVINGS BANK OF
       Plaintiff against KE
                    et    al
Defendant(s).
Pursuant to judgment of foreclosure
and sale entered herein and dated
December 28, 1990. I, the under-
signed Referee will sell at public
auction at the front steps of the
tington Town Hall, 100 Main Street,
                on the 15th day of
         1991 at 10:00 AM premises
beginning at a point on the westerly
side of                  233.85 feet
southerly from the southerly end of
a curve connecting the westerly side
of Katay Drive South (West Katay
Street) with the southerly side of Ef-
fron Avenue, being a plot 100 feet by
200 feet, said premises known as 114
           Drive, Town of

Approximate amount of lien
$147,466.87 plus interest and costs.
Premises will be sold subject to pro-
visions of filed judgement, Index
Number 2918/90. Dated February 11,
1991.                    Re
```

Figure 2.4 A sample legal notice from a newspaper.

3

The Basics of Buying Foreclosures after the Auction— From Banks

The second opportunity to purchase foreclosures is after the auction, when banks (Chapter 3) and government agencies (Chapter 4) sell repossessed foreclosed properties from their inventories.

In Chapter 3 we look at how properties become part of a bank's inventory, why banks are so highly motivated to sell them, and the step-by-step negotiating strategies that help you cut through the red tape and rise above your competition. Sources of bank foreclosure lists are detailed to help you get started. Finally, to give you a more global perspective, buying foreclosures from a bank's inventory is compared and contrasted with buying foreclosures at bank auctions.

Defining Bank-Owned Properties

There are two basic ways that a property becomes bank-owned; (1) the property was not sold at the public auction, and (2) the deed to the property was turned over to the lender by the owners as an alternative to foreclosure.

The Property Was Not Sold at the Auction

Sometimes, nobody shows up to bid on a property that is being sold at an auction. Here are some of the most common reasons for this outcome.

Perhaps the opening bid amount exceeded the public's perceived value of the property, and therefore, it was not considered a good buy. For example, if the liens, judgments, legal fees, and other costs bring the upset price of a property up to $225,000, and the market value is only $200,000, then this would obviously *not* be a property to bid on.

Another reason why a property was not sold at an auction is because a forecast of severe storms and/or other potentially dangerous weather conditions kept bidders from attending.

One more reason why a property is not sold is because it was not publicized properly and the bidding public was unaware of the date and/or time, and/or location of the auction.

When the property is not sold at the auction, the bank "buys it back" for the upset price, and it becomes part of the bank's inventory.

The Deed to the Property
Was Returned to the Lender
(a.k.a. a "Friendly" Foreclosure)

Sometimes a property never reaches the auction because the owner, experiencing (or anticipating) severe financial hardship, works out an agreement with the lender to turn over the deed (and the keys) in exchange for a full release of the remaining mortgage obligation. This procedure is called giving *"a deed in lieu of foreclosure."* It is also known as a *friendly foreclosure.* While lenders <u>are not</u> obligated to accept the deed in lieu of foreclosure, if the value of the property is equal to the outstanding mortgage balance, it makes sense for the lender to bypass the unnecessary expense and time that will be expended to initiate the procedure. The delinquent owner benefits by minimizing the damage to his or her credit rating and eliminating the risk of a *deficiency judgment* if the auction fails to produce enough money to cover the outstanding mortgage balance, whereby if the property sells for more than the outstanding mortgage balance, the delinquent owner forfeits its right to receive any overage (also known as surplus) which would go to the lender that accepted the deed in lieu of foreclosure. (Please note that deficiency judgments may not apply in trust deed states.)

There is also, however, a downside to this strategy for the delinquent owner whereby if the property sells for more than the outstanding mortgage balance, the delinquent owner forfeits the right to receive any overage (also known as surplus), which would go to the lender that accepted the deed in lieu of foreclosure.

Redefining Bank-Owned
Properties

If a property is not sold at the auction, or the lender accepts the deed "in lieu of foreclosure," the lender takes title to the property, and the property becomes part of its inventory. Some lenders call the properties in their inventories "REOs" (<u>R</u>eal-<u>E</u>state-<u>O</u>wned), others call them "OREs" (<u>O</u>wned <u>R</u>eal <u>E</u>state), and some lenders simply call them "bank-owned" real estate.*

* In this book, the terms *"lender" and "bank"* are used interchangeably.

A Lender's View of
Bank-Owned Property

The foreclosure "stigma" that conjured up an image of an evil banker with a black cape, moustache, and top hat is a long-forgotten memory. Lending institutions have become reluctant property owners, charged with the overwhelming task of managing, marketing, and selling the repossessed properties in their inventories. Here are five reasons why foreclosures are a lender's nightmare.

Problem #1—Property damage.   If the house is vacant, it is sitting in the bank's inventory, waiting to be vandalized. In areas with colder climates, the winter months pose an additional threat of frozen pipes unless the property is "winterized"—another expense. And we all know how quickly word gets around when there is a vacant house in the neighborhood. The property could easily become a hangout for local teenagers and a target for break-ins.

Problem #2—Overhead expenses.   The lender is responsible for paying the monthly expenses for the upkeep and maintenance of each property in its inventory until the property is sold. These expenses include homeowner's insurance (to cover the risk of fire damage and other property-related claims), liability insurance (to protect the bank if someone is hurt on the premises), property taxes, lawn care, snow removal, real estate appraisal fees (for estimates of market value), and real estate broker fees (for managing and selling the property)—just to name a few! To provide a context here, one REO specialist for a major lender told me that it cost one million dollars <u>per month</u> to cover the expenses for the 500 properties in his inventory!

Problem #3—Money must be held in reserve to cover "nonperforming assets." When a borrower defaults on a mortgage loan, the foreclosing lender considers the property to be a "nonperforming asset." Federal banking regulations require banks to hold money in reserve to cover the expenses for the nonperforming assets in their inventories. (Personally, I've always thought that they should be called "non-performing *liabilities*" because of the losses that they incur.) Banks conduct business by charging interest on money they lend out. However, if they are unable to make loans because their funds must be held in reserve to cover their nonperforming assets, lenders cannot conduct business. Thus, lenders are highly motivated to sell the properties quickly.

So, to attract buyers, why don't lenders advertise lists of their REO addresses in the major newspapers? They could even implement promotional events and use catchy marketing headlines. For example:

> **Overstocked—Must Sell Our Inventory to Make Room for New Properties**

Or how about:

> **Year-End Clearance—Buy 2 Foreclosures and Get the 3d One For ½ Price**

The answer is that the lending institutions are stuck in a "catch-22" situation. Here's why.

Problem #4—Advertising a supply of foreclosures would be harmful to the lender's public image. If a lender listed the addresses of the foreclosures in its inventory, people would never want to apply to that lender for a mortgage loan. They would be afraid that the lender would publicize *their* addresses if *they* fell behind in *their* payments, and they wouldn't want all of their friends to know that they were having financial problems. Furthermore, a large inventory of foreclosures could make the lender's financial position appear shaky, and people might hesitate to deposit money with a lender that appears to be unstable.

The lenders are better off bypassing the newspaper advertising campaign. But wait a minute! As long as they have to get rid of the properties quickly, why not just sell them for 50 cents on the dollar?

This brings us to Problem #5.

Problem # 5—Federal regulations prohibit "dumping" in a neighborhood. It is well established that the appraised values of properties in a local marketplace are determined by the sales prices of similar properties nearby that were sold recently. Consequently, selling foreclosures for pennies on the dollar (a.k.a. "dumping" the property by selling it for a below-market price) would negatively impact the value of the other homes in that area.

Solution: The best solution—and the one that lenders have used, and continue to use successfully—is to offer incredibly favorable financing terms to attract people who wish to buy foreclosures from the lenders' inventories. The result is deeply discounted interest rates and points, reductions in closing costs, and other loan features that borrowers can't find anywhere else!

An REO Purchase versus a Bank Auction Purchase

The differences between purchasing a foreclosure property at a bank auction and purchasing a bank-owned property from a lender's inventory can vary from lender to lender and from state to state.

Clear title. If you purchase a property at an auction, you may be responsible for unexpected liens and judgments (see Chapter 2). By contrast, most bank-owned properties are sold with clear title. The lending institution usually satisfies any outstanding liens and judgments when the property is taken into its inventory.

The asking price. The manner in which the asking price is established is another factor that distinguishes an auction foreclosure from a bank-owned foreclosure.. While property sold at a bank auction can have an upset price of <u>less than</u> market value because it is set at the unpaid mortgage balance plus the back taxes, court costs, legal fees, etc., a lending institution will base the asking price of bank-owned property on market value. To illustrate this concept, if the market value of a property is $200,000 and the unpaid mortgage balance plus accumulated charges (including court costs, legal fees, and back taxes) totals $180,000, the opening bid amount at the auction would be $180,000. On the other hand, if the property is not sold at the auction and the lender has to take it back into its inventory and sell it as an REO, the asking price of the property would be $200,000.

Evicting the occupants. If you purchase a property at a foreclosure auction, you are responsible for evicting any occupants after you become the new owner. Conversely, the REO seller may have evicted the occupants from its bank-owned property, thereby eliminating the time and expense of eviction procedures.

Presenting your offer. When you purchase a property at a foreclosure auction, the offers are usually communicated through the process of verbal bidding. By contrast, offers for a bank-owned property are usually submitted in writing to the lender (or to the lender's real estate broker).

Seller financing. When you purchase a property at a bank auction, the referee does not provide financing—you pay for the property with *cash,* or arrange for financing independently through a lending institution. In comparison, when you purchase a bank-owned property, you can usually negotiate attractive financing terms with the lending institution that owns it and also happens to be the seller. Remember that it costs a lot of money for the upkeep of bank-owned property, and it is beneficial for bank-owned property sellers to offer favorable financing terms as an incentive—to sell the property quickly.

"As is" condition. Unlike a foreclosure auction, where properties are purchased in "as is" condition, when you purchase a bank-owned property from a lending institution, the lending institution may agree to give you credit towards making necessary structural repairs. This is because a bank does not want the negative publicity that could come back to it if, for example, someone who just purchased a foreclosure from XXX Bank the previous week was seriously hurt when the cesspool caved in.

Figure 3-1 compares and contrasts the basic distinctions between purchasing a foreclosure at a bank auction and purchasing an REO from a bank's inventory.

Finding REOs

Lending Institutions

Years ago, lending institutions would not admit that they had repossessed properties in their inventories. As we discussed earlier in this chapter, it could hurt a lender's public image for potential borrowers to think that the lending institution would take drastic action (such as foreclosing) if borrowers didn't pay their mortgages. Today, however, because of the vast numbers of properties in their inventories, many lending institutions have "come out of the closet," and are willing to admit openly that they have bank-owned foreclosures available for sale. Some lenders even prepare lists of their bank-owned properties with attractive financing terms to make the properties easier to buy.

You can contact lenders and ask for their foreclosure department or their asset-recovery division, asset liquidation departments, REO or ORE departments, or whatever departments are in charge of their bank-owned property. Ask them to send you a list of their available properties and information about the bidding procedures you must follow in order to purchase their properties.

Web Sites

Most lending institutions use Web sites to advertise the services they provide for their customers, and you may find information posted there about foreclosures. The information generally includes the

A BANK AUCTION PURCHASE VERSUS AN REO PURCHASE	
BUYING A FORECLOSURE AT A BANK AUCTION	BUYING AN REO FROM A BANK OR GOVERNMENT AGENCY'S INVENTORY
1. The asking price is based on the unpaid mortgage balance plus expenses.	1. The asking price is based on market value.
2. The referee who sells the property at the auction does not provide financing.	2. The REO seller may provide financing terms that are extremey favorable for a buyer.
3. The burden of evicting the current occupants is on the new owner, after title is conveyed.	3. The REO seller may already have evicted the occupants before the property was placed on the market.
4. The plumbing, heating, electrical systems, and the appliances and roof are sold in "as is" condition.	4. The REO seller may agree to pay for repairs if structural damage is discovered.
5. The manner of making an offer to purchase the property is by verbal bidding at a public auction.	5. The manner of making an offer to purchase the property is by written offer to the REO seller.
6. The new owner may be responsible for unexpected liens and judgments on the premises, in addition to the purchase price.	6. The REO seller usually clears up any existing title problems before title is conveyed to the new owner.

Figure 3-1. A bank auction purchase vs. an REO purchase.

property addresses, the asking prices, access to the properties, pictures of the properties, information about the property taxes, lot sizes, and contact information for access to the properties.

Real Estate Offices

Another source of foreclosure listings is your local real estate company. Most lending institutions do not have the property management capabilities, or the staffing to manage, repair, advertise, and show the properties in their inventories to buyers. After all, banks are not in the business of selling real estate; their function is to lend money to people who want to buy real estate. As a result, in many cases lending institutions give listings of their bank-owned properties to local real estate brokers, The real estate professionals advertise the properties, show them to prospective buyers, present offers to the lender and, if the property is sold, the lender pays the broker's fee.

Word of Mouth/Observation

One more very viable source of REO properties is through the grapevine—from friends or family, or from acquaintances who know someone that was foreclosed on by a bank, or who know of a house in their neighborhood that was recently boarded up by a bank. In some cases, you may coincidentally come upon a bank-owned property while you are driving around in a town where you would like to own a home. In those cases, a sign may have been posted with the name of the bank that owns the property, and a telephone number to contact for more information. If no sign is posted, the next door neighbors are good sources of information, and can usually tell you something that can help you find the owner.

Preparing Your Offer

More often than not, the list from the lending institution that is selling the property includes the asking price. You <u>should</u> <u>not</u> assume that this price is "set in stone." When you are ready to make your offer, you will do so based on the price that is best for you. (Inspection techniques are covered in Chapter 9, and instructions for preparing a bid sheet are covered in Chapter 10.) Remember two important things:

#1) The properties are sitting in the lender's inventory, costing the bank money, and #2) You are dealing with a highly motivated seller.

Offer Letter for a Bank-Owned Property

Today's Date:

XYZ Bank
000 Smith Street
Anytown, U.S.A. 00000

Attn: Foreclosure Department

Dear _____ :

With reference to the property located at _____,
I would like to submit the following offer:

    Purchase price:

    Down payment:

    Financing terms:

    Closing date:

    Amount enclosed (deposit/binder):

Please contact me at your earliest convenience with your acceptance.

The best time to contact me is between _____and _____.

My telephone number is: (____) _____ .

My current address is:

Very truly yours,

(Your Name)

Figure 3-2. An example of an offer letter for a bank-owned property.

The offer you make should be in writing, and it should be as specific as possible. Here are the most important items to include:

The address. Clearly indicate the exact address of the property you wish to purchase. The lending institution may have assigned identification numbers to the properties in its inventory, and you should include that number as well.

The purchase price. Your offer should include the purchase price, that is, the amount of money you are offering to pay for the property.

The deposit. Some lending institutions may require you to send in a deposit (also called a *binder*) along with your offer. The deposit is usually a nominal amount ($100) that will be refunded or returned to you if your offer is not accepted. If your offer is accepted, the lending institution keeps your deposit and applies it to the purchase price.

The financing terms. If you want the lender to provide you with financing for the property, your offer should include the financing terms including the interest rate you wish to pay, the amount you want to borrow, and the length of time of the mortgage (usually 15, 20, or 30 years).

The down payment. If the lending institution you are purchasing the property from is providing financing, the difference between the amount they will lend you and the purchase price, is called the "*down payment.*" Your offer should include that number.

The closing date. Your offer should stipulate the day you wish to take title (ownership) and possession.

Your contact information. Be certain to have your name, address, and telephone number on the letter so that a representative from the lending institution can contact you with a decision regarding your offer.

Figure 3-2 is an example of an offer letter for a bank-owned property.

Negotiating Strategies That Help You Cut through the Red Tape

Justify Low Offers with Documentation

Keep in mind that lending institutions must price bank-owned properties at "market value" to prevent the negative impact that underpricing would have on the values of other properties in the neighborhood. There are, however, extenuating circumstances—specifically, the substandard condition of a property—that legitimately affects the market value, and, as a result, justifies a deeply discounted sales price.

It is possible that, in some cases, a property is priced at a ridiculously high amount. This could just be a mistake on the part of the appraiser.

Another explanation is that the appraisal was initially prepared a while ago, when the property first went into the bank's inventory, and when it *had* a kitchen. Since then, the property may have been vandalized and, as a result, the value is substantially reduced. If you want to purchase the property, don't just send in a low offer with a note that the amount you are offering to pay is low because "the property needs a lot of work." Instead, take pictures of the vandalized rooms to accurately illustrate its present condition, (i.e., the fact that most of the kitchen has been gutted), and send the pictures with estimates from two contractors along with your offer. By doing so, you are helping the lender justify its decision to accept an offer that is lower than what it thought was market value.

Rise Above Your Competition

There are likely to be several people submitting offers simultaneously for the same property that you are interested in. What do you have that would be highly regarded by a lender, and that would give you an edge over your competitors if their offers are for similar amounts? The answer is "an outstanding credit report."

First, with excellent credit, there is a greater likelihood that you will be able to obtain financing, either from the lender that is selling this property, or from another financial institution, without the customary delays that can accompany a questionable credit history. This will help expedite the sales process and removal of the property from the lender's inventory.

Second, an outstanding credit rating is indicative of your willingness and ability to pay your mortgage in a timely fashion, which means that if your offer is accepted, the owner of the bank-owned property doesn't have to worry that the property will return to its inventory in the near future.

You can call and inquire as to which of the credit report providers the lender prefers. Obtain a copy of your credit report from the reporting agency (or agencies) and submit it along with your written offer. Your diligence in maintaining a great credit rating is something to be proud of, and it makes good business sense to use this hard-earned resource to your advantage.

4

The Basics of Buying Foreclosures after the Auction—From Federal, State, and Local Government Agencies

In Chapter 3 we looked at buying bank-owned foreclosures after the auction. We expand on this multifaceted opportunity in Chapter 4, as we tap into another source of repossessed properties—federal, state and local government agencies. The manner in which a property becomes part of each government agency's inventory is also included for general background information.

Defining Government-Owned Property

Federal, state, and local governments have a variety of residential, commercial and industrial foreclosed properties in their inventories. Each agency's specifications for bidders to inspect these properties and submit offers to purchase them are clearly detailed in their pamphlets, on their Web sites, and in bidding packages that they send out to people who request them. In most cases, the lists include the asking price, but as noted in Chapter 3, when you are ready to make your offer, you will do so based on the price that is best for you. Also as noted in Chapter 3, we cover inspection techniques that apply to all types of foreclosures in Chapter 9, and instructions for preparing a bid sheet are reviewed in Chapter 10.

The rest of this chapter details the names and contact information for the government agencies.

Government Services Administration (GSA) Sales

The Government Services Administration (GSA) Property Disposition Offices oversee the sale of real estate that was formerly used by the federal government. The list includes office buildings, vacant land, high-rise buildings, residential homes previously occupied by military families and residential property that was confiscated by law enforcement officials.

The U.S. government offers these surplus properties to the general public through a system of public bidding in order to increase tax revenues. An invitation for bids (IFB) is prepared for each property that is sold. The IFB includes directions to the property and instructions on who to contact for inspecting the property prior to bidding.

Telephone contact: To find out about upcoming sales, contact your local General Services Administration Office and ask for the *U.S. Real Property Sales List.*

Internet (www) contact: You can access the *U.S. Real Property Sales List* and the GSA Official Bid Forms through the *Property Disposal* Web page on the GSA.gov Web site.

Department of Housing and Urban Development (HUD) Sales (a.k.a. FHA Foreclosures)

The U.S. Department of Housing and Urban Development (HUD) sales, also known as Federal Housing Administration (FHA) foreclosures, occur when a borrower defaults and the lender forecloses on an FHA loan. HUD pays the lending institution for the outstanding loan and expenses incurred. HUD takes ownership and resells the property to the public.

HUD guidelines require buyers to go through HUD's designated real estate brokers in order to inspect and bid on the foreclosures HUD sells. HUD provides buyers with a list of designated brokers to contact for information about properties they are interested in purchasing. The HUD area broker prepares the buyer's bids and submits them to HUD. Sealed bids are accepted by mail, and must include a 10-percent down payment. HUD will pay the real estate broker's commission if the offer is accepted.

In many cases, HUD will provide lower interest mortgages for these properties, but purchasers may be required to live in the house and not rent it out to others for a specified period (i.e., three years).

Newspaper: HUD often posts upcoming auction information in local newspapers on a weekly basis. Figure 4-1 is an illustration of a HUD advertisement.

Telephone contact: To find out more about upcoming HUD/FHA sales and the designated HUD brokers in your area, contact your local HUD Office.

Internet (www) contact: You can access HUD Homes on the Surplus/ Excess Properties Web page on the *Department of Housing and Urban Development.gov* Web site.

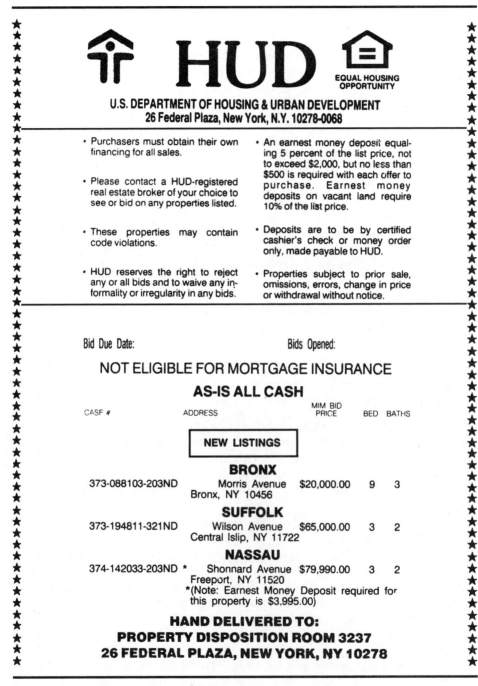

Figure 4-1. An illustration of an HUD advertisement.

Veterans Administration
(VA) Sales

Veterans Administration sales occur when the Department of Veteran's Affairs (DVA) repossesses property from a serviceman or servicewoman who has been foreclosed on. You are *not* required to be a serviceperson or even an *owner-occupant* (someone who will buy the property to live in and not use it as a rental property) to purchase these properties. The VA utilizes the services of local real estate brokers to sell the properties to the public. The brokers are responsible for showing the properties to prospective buyers and preparing purchase offers. The VA pays the broker's commission.

The VA offers favorable financing terms for many VA–owned properties. Successful high bidders must satisfy steady employment and good credit criteria.

Telephone contact: To find out more about VA-owned foreclosures, call your local Department of Veterans Affairs Office and ask for information about the *Home Loan Guaranty Services.*

Internet (www) Contact: You can access VA-owned foreclosures on the *Home Loan Guaranty Services* Web page on the *Department of Veterans Affairs.gov* Web site.

Federal Deposit Insurance
Corp. (FDIC) Sales

The Federal Deposit Insurance Corporation is an independent agency of the U.S. government. While best known as a provider of the insurance that protects savings and checking account depositors in U.S. banks, the FDIC also functions in the role of its predecessor, the Resolution Trust Corporation, as the Receiver when an insured financial institution fails.

In its role as Receiver, the FDIC pays out the insured deposits to the failed institution customers directly, or transfers the deposits to another financial institution, where depositors can gain immediate access to their funds.

In its role as a government-owned foreclosure seller, the FDIC provides lists of properties from its inventory for purchasers who are interested in buying residential and commercial property, and vacant land.

Telephone contact: To find out more about FDIC-owned foreclosures, call your local FDIC Office and ask for information about *Real Estate Property For Sale.*

Internet (www) contact: You can access FDIC–owned foreclosures on the *Buying From and Selling To The FDIC* Web page on the FDIC.gov Web site.

Federal Home Loan Mortgage Corp. (Freddie Mac) Sales

The Federal Home Loan Mortgage Corp. (Freddie Mac) is a publicly chartered agency that buys residential mortgages from lending institutions. Freddie Mac sells its foreclosures through real estate brokers who manage the properties in each state. Freddie Mac prefers selling to owner-occupants, but also works with investors. HomeSteps Asset Services is the unit that markets foreclosed homes for Freddie Mac, and provides special financing for qualified purchasers of Freddie Mac-owned properties.

Telephone contact: To find out more about Freddie Mac-owned foreclosures, call your local Freddie Mac Office and ask for information about *HomeSteps Foreclosure Listings.*

Internet (www) contact: You can access Freddie Mac-owned foreclosures on the *HomeSteps.com* Web site.

Federal National Mortgage Association (Fannie Mae) Sales

The Federal National Mortgage Association (Fannie Mae) is the largest purchaser of mortgages in the secondary market. Fannie Mae offers financing incentives to qualified buyers through its staff of HomePath Specialists. Fannie Mae hires real estate brokers to sell the foreclosures in its inventory. A list of Fannie Mae-owned foreclosures with property information and the names and contact information for the real estate brokers is available by telephone and on the Internet.

Telephone contact: To find out more about Fannie Mae-owned property, call your local Fannie Mae Public Information Office and ask for information about *Foreclosure Listings.*

Internet (www) contact: You can access Fannie Mae foreclosures on its Web site at *Fanniemae.com.*

5

The Basics of Buying Foreclosures before the Auction

In Chapter 5 we explore the third opportunity to purchase foreclosures, where buyers help delinquent homeowners* avoid foreclosure by purchasing property directly from them before the auction commences.

Delinquent homeowners benefit from pre-auction purchases because they can preserve their credit ratings and avoid the risk of incurring additional debt. Buyers benefit from pre-auction purchases because they can buy a property before the costs associated with foreclosure proceedings drive up the purchase price.

---

* In this chapter, *"delinquent homeowners"* and *"delinquent owners"* are people who have fallen behind in paying their mortgages, and who are anywhere from one day late, up until such time as the foreclosure action is completed and they have forfeited their interest in the property.

Understanding the Delinquent Owners

Before you start to knock on the doors of people who are facing fore-closure, it is important to understand the psychological effect that the pending foreclosure may be having on them. It is also good to know the other alternatives that are available to them, the viability of those options, and the time frame within which decisions must be made so that you can accurately organize your plan of action.

As a purchaser of foreclosures for myself and for other investors, I met a lot of people who were trying to sell their homes to avoid fore-closure. In response to my questions as to what caused them to fall so far behind in making their mortgage payments, some people said that injuries or illnesses caused them to lose a lot of time from work, some others were laid off. In many cases, divorce had taken its toll. Some peo-ple had taken an equity loan to start a business that failed, and that extra monetary obligation was choking them each month. But by far, the most prevalent causes were denial and procrastination. People just didn't believe it could happen to them. They "put their heads in the sand" and figured that somehow, somewhere, someone would bail them out before they lost their homes.

How You Can Help

If you feel uncomfortable about contacting people who are being fore-closed on, it may help you to know that you may be their last (and best) alternative to the menacing threat of foreclosure that is, in most cases, inevitable. For many delinquent homeowners, the property has become an albatross, a heavy burden that they can't afford to keep and are unable to sell.

If you can negotiate an agreement to purchase the property and the transaction takes place before the lender sells it at a foreclosure auc-tion, there are four important ways that you can change their lives.

First, you can help them save some equity, so they don't lose everything. Depending on the condition of the property, and general market con-ditions, if you are paying them even a small amount of money above their mortgage balance, it may be more than they would have ended up with if the property went to auction.

Second, you can help them save their credit. If the property is sold before the auction is held, the delinquent owners' credit reports will show late mortgage payments, but will not reflect the stigma of a foreclosure sale (the effects of which can damage their credit rating for years to come). This is a very valuable result, especially if the delinquent owners would like to relocate to a more affordable area, with a lower cost of living, and where they can buy another home in the near future.

Third, you can help them avoid losing future income. If the property ends up in foreclosure, and it is not sold at the auction, it becomes a bank-owned property in the lender's inventory. If it is subsequently sold for less than the amount that was owed, the foreclosing lender could file a deficiency judgment against the delinquent owners for the difference. For example, let's say two homeowners (husband and wife) fall behind on their mortgage payments and the lender brings a foreclosure action. If the upset price for the delinquent owners' house (including legal fees, back interest, late charges, and court costs) totals $200,000, and it is subsequently sold for $140,000, the foreclosing lender could file a defi-ciency judgment against the delinquent homeowners for the $60,000 difference. A deficiency judgment could result in garnished wages, and, depending on state law, if the delinquent homeowners have other assets, they can be seized and sold to pay off the outstanding balance owed to the foreclosing lender.

Fourth, you can prevent this from getting even uglier. To continue our example from the previous paragraph, in most cases, the delinquent homeowners do not have any other assets that the foreclosing lender can seize. The lender may also encounter problems garnishing the wages of people without jobs. If it cannot recover the $60,000 loss in assets, the foreclosing lender "writes it off" by sending the delinquent homeowners a 1099 tax form in the amount of $60,000. The consequences to the delinquent homeowners are devastating. Not only did they lose their home, but now they also owe federal income taxes, and, if applicable, state, city, and other local income taxes on the $60,000 that they never even had the benefit of enjoying.

Negotiating with Delinquent Owners—When the Property Has Equity

Before you try to buy a property from delinquent owners, it is helpful to be aware of some of the other options available to them for avoiding foreclosure, and to have some insight as to which of these options may or may not be viable. In the following situations, if delinquent owners reject your offer to purchase the property from them initially, your best negotiation strategy may simply be to give the delinquent owners your contact number so that they can reach you if the other options they are relying on to avoid foreclosure cannot be brought to fruition.

Option #1. They can sell the property on the open market. Quite often, the delinquent owners are trying to sell the house to avoid foreclosure, but they have it listed for too much money, even though they risk losing everything if they can't sell it before the lender forecloses.

If the delinquent owners are not responsive and resist your attempts to talk to them about selling to you, just give them your business card, or write your name and contact number on a piece of paper for them. Touch base with them periodically (i.e., every other week or so) to ask if they have been successful in their attempts to sell the house. *Remember that the delinquent owners still own the property – up until the auction begins.* This means that they still have the right to avoid foreclosure by selling the property before the auction commences.

Option #2. They can file for bankruptcy. Another way people save their homes from foreclosure is to file for bankruptcy. What these people may not know is that homeowners who file for bankruptcy are still responsible for paying the mortgage each month or the property will be released from the protection of the bankruptcy court and sold to satisfy creditors. Also, some forms of bankruptcy require a reorganization plan for debt consolidation and repayment, and the plan may be turned down by the courts if the people lack sufficient income to repay those debts in accordance with the plan.

Option #3. They are applying for a "hard-money" loan. Some delinquent homeowners borrow money and use it to bring their monthly mortgage payments current. A hard-money loan is different from "break-your-arm" financing by a loan shark. Hard-money lenders traditionally charge much higher interest rates and a greater amount of points than conventional lenders, and the borrower must have a source of income in order to pay the loan back. This may, once again, pose a problem for the home-owners whose delinquency is the result of a job loss.

Option #4. They can work out a payment plan with the lender. Another alternative available to the delinquent homeowner is to work out a pay-ment plan with the foreclosing lender. But, there is a possibility that payment plans had already been defaulted on by the borrowers, and the foreclosing lender may not be willing to extend any more deadlines.

Option #5. They will give the foreclosing lender the deed "in lieu of foreclo-sure" and leave. As discussed in Chapter 3, the homeowners can ask the lender to accept the deed in lieu of foreclosure. If the lender agrees, the homeowners give the lender the deed and the keys to the property to prevent the foreclosure sale, and the transaction is considered an even exchange. Be aware that this alternative may not be available if the lender does not agree to it. Also, be aware that once the property is accepted into the bank's inventory, if it subsequently sells for more money than the outstanding balance, the overage will not be credited back to the delinquent owners.

Negotiating with Delinquent Owners—When There Is Negative Equity (a.k.a. "Short Sales")

Sometimes the delinquent owners are unable to sell the property because, after the foreclosure has begun and legal fees, interest charges, etc., have been added to the unpaid mortgage balance, the owners may have to sell the property for more than it is worth in order to pay off the loan. That is, of course, assuming that they can sell the house before it fore-closes. This situation most frequently occurs when the market values of real estate depreciate, especially when the property was highly leveraged to begin with (i.e., the buyers put very little money down as a down-payment and took out a large mortgage loan). And if the inflated sales price doesn't make it impossible to sell, the fact that the property is probably in less than "stellar" condition (due to the owner's financial difficulties) will probably do the trick.

When the mortgage balance exceeds the value of the property, what many people don't realize is that the lending institutions can, and, in many circumstances, do agree to accept *less than* the outstanding mortgage balance as payment in full. This arrangement is called a *short sale* (where the proceeds of the property sale fall *short* of the amount needed to pay off the mortgage balance). It is also known as a *cram down* (where the lender *crams down* the outstanding balance of the loan so that it is in conformity with the real market value of the property).

Even though the property still legally belongs to the delinquent homeowner until the auction cuts off his or her interests, there is one circumstance where the lender must be included in the sales negotiations. That situation arises when the delinquent owner agrees to sell the property for an amount less than the outstanding mortgage balance. Because the lender is financially affected by the transaction, it has to be a part of the negotiations and must agree to the short sale.

The lender has a good reason to work with the delinquent owner in this circumstance. Accepting your lower offer may cost the lender a few thousand dollars now, but that initial "investment" will save the lender many thousands of dollars in the long run. Why? Because if you don't buy it, the property will be auctioned at the higher upset price (inflated with back taxes, legal fees, interest, etc.), and since that price exceeds market value, it is unlikely that anyone will buy it at the auction. The property will then become a nonperforming asset in the lender's portfolio, and the lender will incur all of the extra expenses for the upkeep and maintenance of the premises, including property insurance and liability coverage, property taxes, etc. Finally, to add insult to injury, the lender will have to lower the asking price in order to sell it for market value, and ultimately, at the end of the day, the amount that it sold for will probably be equal (or less than) what you originally offered!

If you can reach an agreement with the delinquent owners, you may be able to negotiate with the foreclosing lender directly. This is especially true when the auction date is looming and time is of the essence, and where the delinquent owners are unsophisticated about the concept of short sales and intimidated by the prospect of trying to negotiate with the foreclosing lender on their own behalf. The foreclosing lender will most likely require the delinquent owners to sign a form called a *"waiver of confidentiality"* (or its equivalent) which gives the foreclosing lender formal, written permission to discuss the loan with the party named on the document.

As part of the contract preparations, you should request confirmation *in writing* from the foreclosing lender that the amount you have agreed to pay as the purchase price will also be considered "payment in full" for the outstanding mortgage balance.

Finding "Pre-Auction" Foreclosures

There are several sources that are available to you for finding people who are in default on their mortgage loans and who are facing foreclosure.

"Legal Notices" in Local Newspapers

In many states, the foreclosure procedures require public notice prior to the auction. Upcoming auctions are frequently advertised in the "legal notices" section in local newspapers.

Legal notices usually include the property address, the legal description, and the date, time and location of the auction. A sample legal notice can be found in Chapter 2, Figure 2-4.

Lis Pendens Lists

Banks will not publicize information about delinquent loans until the borrowers are in default and the foreclosure action commences. The manner in which the foreclosure action proceeds is usually guided by state statute, as discussed in Chapter 1. In states where the foreclosure process is initiated by the filing of a *notice of pending action* (a.k.a. *lis pendens*) with the court, the documents are considered to be public notice, and they can be accessed at the county clerk's office in the county where the property is located.

There are also companies that sell *lis pendens* lists. You can look up the names of such companies on the Internet, and in reference books in your local library. Sometimes the publishers of upcoming auction lists offer *lis pendens* lists as an additional accommodation to give their subscribers a chance to buy properties "before" as well as "at" an auction.

Local Real Estate Offices

When homeowners face severe enough financial difficulties that they must sell their homes quickly to avoid losing everything, they may reach out to their local real estate company for assistance. You can visit local real estate offices and ask the real estate professionals who work there to keep your name on file as someone who is interested in buying pre-auction properties.

Contacting Delinquent Owners

When contacting delinquent homeowners, be aware that they may still be in a state of denial and may not even wish to speak to you. If this happens, patient, compassionate persistence will be your key to success. Here are some techniques that can help you communicate and negotiate more effectively with delinquent owners.

Once Is Not Enough

It has been my experience that, in most cases, the typical delinquent homeowners will not show interest in your offer to buy the property until the *fifth* time you contact them. Timing is everything. When the delinquent owners decide that it is time to act, you want to be the first person they turn to. For optimum results, call or send a letter (see below) approximately once every three weeks.

Dress for Success

If you are planning to meet with the delinquent homeowners face-to-face, please remember that you are dealing with people who are in financial peril. Should you wear your most expensive jewelry, your designer clothing, and have your airline ticket for a Hawaiian vacation strategically positioned (destination side pointed outward) in your pocket—you know, to assure them that you can afford to do business with them? *Of course not!* Because these people could be losing everything, it would be thoughtless and insensitive to flaunt your good fortune. It is also a foolish business strategy because it almost begs the sellers to negotiate a higher purchase price with you since you obviously can afford it. You are much better off wearing jeans or similarly suitable casual clothing. Above all, the most important things to bring with you are a friendly smile and a compassionate attitude.

Letters That Open Doors

If you feel uncomfortable about approaching the delinquent homeowners on a face-to-face basis initially, send them a letter instead. The letter itself can be typed or handwritten—the main criteria is legibility. If you have great handwriting, write out the letter; if your handwriting stinks (like mine does), type the letter. For a more personal approach, you should address the letter to the homeowner's names rather than to "Dear Occupant." The letter should indicate that you understand the problems they are having, that many, many people are in the same boat, and that they have nothing to be ashamed of. Keep the letter short, simple, and nonthreatening. An example of a letter to delinquent owners is illustrated in Figure 5-1.

Envelopes That Beg to Be Opened

While the most important thing about your letter is that the recipients can read what you wrote, the envelope faces a more daunting challenge;

An Example of a Letter To a Delinquent Owner

Today's Date:

Delinquent Owners Name(s)
000 Smith Street
Anytown, USA 00000

Dear _____

I understand that you are having difficulty making your mortgage payments, as are many people in today's economy.

If you would be interested talking to me about a quick sale, please call me at (   )_____.

The best time to contact me is between the hours of _____ and _____.

Very truly yours,

(Your Name)

Figure 5-1 An example of a letter to a delinquent owner.

it must compel the recipients to open it up and read its contents! We *don't* want the delinquent owners to think that our letter is from a creditor who is threatening to sue them, and, as a result, throw the letter in the garbage without reading it. If that happens, they missed out on what could be their last chance to sell the property before the lender forecloses— simply because they didn't know they had another option.

Begin with a *handwritten, pastel-colored, "invitation-sized"* envelope that cannot possibly be mistaken for a bill from a creditor. At least this way it is more likely that the delinquent owners will read your letter. If they throw it in the garbage after they finish reading it, fine. At least they knew that there were other options available to them when they made their choice.

Remember, if you ever feel tacky or uncomfortable about approaching people who are experiencing financial difficulty, remind yourself that "you can help them," but they have to want to help themselves as well.

Additional Strategies and Tips for Buying Pre-Auction Foreclosures

Include These Contract Terms

If you are successful in reaching an agreement to buy a pre-auction property, your contract with the delinquent owners should be contingent upon the results of a title search. Your attorney can assist you in obtaining this. The search will confirm that there are no extra liens or judgments that you were unaware of, and which, as the new owner, you could be responsible for. *Do not release any money to the delinquent owners until your attorney reviews the title report and assures you that there are no problems.*

Other contract terms include the repairs to the premises, if any, that the delinquent homeowner will complete prior to closing, and the appliances, furnishings and fixtures (i.e., window treatments, air conditioners, carpeting) that are included in the sale of the property.

Use the "B" (as in Bankruptcy) Word in "Self-Defense" if the Lender Is Unreasonable

When a lender begins a foreclosure action, the delinquent owner often tries to sell the property to avoid losing his credit, his equity, and even his future earnings. And, in most cases, a bona fide contract with a purchaser, along with a lender's commitment to finance the premises, is enough of a good-faith effort for a foreclosing lender to agree to postpone the auction for a reasonable period of time—i.e., one or two weeks.

Sometimes, however, the foreclosing lender refuses to postpone the auction, and the sale cannot take place before the auction is held. The alternative for many delinquent owners in this situation is to file for bankruptcy, which temporarily stops the foreclosure from proceeding any further. Sometimes just advising the foreclosing lender that the delinquent owners intend to file for bankruptcy is enough to achieve the intended result—that being the foreclosing lender's cooperation in rescheduling the auction to a later date.

There are, however, *very serious consequences* to be aware of when people chose bankruptcy as an alternative to foreclosure. First, people with a bankruptcy in their credit history can expect to pay higher interest rates on future loans, and there is a strong likelihood that they will even be denied loans until the bankruptcy is discharged and/or new credit has been established. Second, laws that prohibit deed transfers by people who have filed for bankruptcy may cause problems for people who wish to convey the property. The delinquent owner may even be charged additional legal fees to release the property from bankruptcy protection so that it can be sold. Before choosing bankruptcy, delinquent owners should ask their attorneys if there is another remedy besides bankruptcy that allows them to delay the upcoming foreclosure auction so that they can sell the property.

On the other hand, if the delinquent owners are planning to move to another locale where the cost of living is more affordable for them, and they intend to purchase another home shortly—foreclosure could be even more prejudicial than bankruptcy—especially to a prospective lender who does not want to see foreclosure history repeat itself at *his* bank's expense.

Before making any final decisions, it is important for the delinquent owners to seek legal and financial advice regarding bankruptcy and foreclosure options based on their particular circumstances.

6

Financing Foreclosures with Traditional Mortgage Loans

Riddle:

What is the largest purchase most people make during their lifetimes?
A home?
No!
Guess again.
The answer is—a mortgage loan.

Whether you are a first-time foreclosure purchaser, or you are purchasing your third foreclosure, a mortgage loan is the most popular way to finance foreclosures. Unfortunately, for people who are unfamiliar with the loan procedure, applying for a mortgage is more anxiety producing than a medical exam by a proctologist who uses oversized instruments.

Just as you will spend many hours of preparation choosing the property that is right for you, you should take an equal amount of time and care to choose a lender with a mortgage loan that best meets your present monetary needs and your future financial goals. To accomplish this, in Chapter 6 we look at the types of loans available as well as the benefits and risks associated with each type of loan.

The Burden of Proof

The basic concept is simple and straightforward. The idea is to convince a lender to give you, the applicant, money to purchase a real estate property. To accomplish this, two qualifying factors must be proven. First, you must demonstrate that you have sufficient income to repay the loan. Second, in the event that you default on your promise to repay the loan and the lender forecloses, you must document that the real estate property that you pledged as security for the loan has enough value that the lender can recapture its losses at a foreclosure auction. The entire mortgage approval procedure is aimed at defining and proving these two premises.

Decisions, Decisions

While no one has a crystal ball to ascertain what tomorrow will bring, there are some basic purchasing choices you can make (and may already have made) that will help you narrow down your preferences. When you have formulated an overall game plan, you are more likely to select a loan that is compatible with your present financial circumstances and your future economic goals. Here are some choices to consider.

What type of property do you want to purchase?

The major categories of real property are residential, commercial, and industrial. These categories can be broken down further into subcategories. For example, condominiums, cooperatives, single-family homes, two-family homes, apartment buildings, etc., are subcategories of residential property. Someone who wants to purchase a single-family property will have different loan options than someone who wishes to buy an apartment building.

Are you purchasing as an owner-occupant (who will live there) or as an investor (who will rent it out to tenants)?

An owner-occupant will usually receive a more favorable interest rate and lower points than an investor because the lender is taking less of a risk. Whereas a lender can accurately qualify an owner-occupant based on his individual ability to repay the mortgage, the investor's ability to repay the mortgage is strongly influenced by the financial strength of a tenant that the investor has selected and that the lender has not qualified. In Chapter 8 we compare investor loans with loans for owner-occupants in much greater detail (also see Figure 8-1).

How long do you intend to own the property?

Pinpointing your future ownership plans, that is, the length of time you wish to own the property, can help you select the most beneficial mortgage loan for you. For example, if you intend to keep the property for more than five years, you will probably be better off with a fixed-rate mortgage that will remain the same over the life of the loan. On the other hand, if you are buying the property with the intention of reselling it in less than five years (i.e, fixing up a handyman's special and selling it when the repairs are complete), you may be better off with a variable (adjustable) rate mortgage loan. The variable rate loan usually begins with a lower initial rate than a fixed-rate loan, and the premises will be sold *before* periodic increases elevate the interest rate higher than a fixed rate.

How many years do you want the mortgage to last before it is paid off ?

The length of the loan term, (i.e., a 15-year mortgage, a 30-year mortgage) usually influences the loan's interest rate, the monthly mortgage payment, and the borrower's equity. In comparing a 15-year mortgage with a 30-year mortgage, generally a 15-year loan has a quicker equity build-up and a lower interest rate, but the monthly mortgage payment is higher than it would be for a 30-year loan. The differences between 15- and 30-year loans are discussed in more detail later on in this chapter.

Will you apply for a conventional loan or a government-backed loan?

In return for deep discounts on interest rates, points, and other loan costs, government-backed loans may have more restrictive qualifying criteria than conventional loans. Government loans may have guidelines that regulate the purchase price of the property, the amount of the down-payment, the amount of family income, the length of time the borrower pledges to occupy the property, whether or not the applicant is required to be a first time buyer, etc. Government-backed loans are discussed in more detail later on in this chapter.

Are you interested in buying a "handyman's special" or a property that is already in "move-in condition"?

Some lenders require verification from its own representatives that the plumbing, heating, and electrical systems are operable before approving the loans. Someone who is purchasing a handyman's special could face lengthy delays in obtaining financing under those circumstances, and should apply for a loan with a lender that does not "condition" its loan approval on the "condition" of the property.

Types of Mortgage Loans

The following section will help applicants understand the different types of mortgage loans that are available.

Conventional Fixed-Rate Mortgages

The first type of loan is a fixed-rate mortgage with monthly interest payments that do not fluctuate for the life of the loan. Conventional 30-year mortgage loans offer absolute certainty on housing costs (aside from annual increases in property taxes and/or homeowner's insurance premiums). Conventional 15-year mortgage loans have lower interest rates than 30-year loans because the quicker payoff allows a lender to put the money to work again sooner by lending it to a new borrower.

Figure 6-1 illustrates the outcome when the same amount of money is borrowed for a 15-year term compared to a 30-year term. Borrower A's $50,000 mortgage is amortized over 30 years at a 12-percent interest rate, and the monthly principal and interest payment is $514.31. Borrower B's $50,000 mortgage, amortized over 15 years, has a reduced interest rate (anywhere from one-quarter to one-half of a percent lower). At 11½-percent interest, the monthly principal and interest payment is $584.09, or $69.78 per month more than Borrower A's monthly payment. Borrower B's higher monthly payment requires more provable income than Borrower A must show, but Borrower B's 15-year mortgage offers faster equity buildup and quicker payoff of the loan than Borrower A's 30-year mortgage. If you were to freeze the mortgage loan accounts of Borrower A and Borrower B after 5 years, the differences between their 15- and 30-year mortgages are quite significant.

Borrower B's monthly payment is only $69.78 more per month than Borrower A's payment, yet, after five years, Borrower B has paid off $8455.19 on the 15-year loan compared to $1168.70 paid off by Borrower A on the 30-year loan.

There is an obvious benefit in choosing the 15-year mortgage, but many people are reluctant to commit to the higher monthly payments. Those who choose the 30-year loan due to the lower monthly payments can still reduce the term of the loan by making extra payments during the year without committing to the higher monthly payment required for the 15-year loan. (When making extra payments, you should include clear instructions for the lender to apply the additional amounts to the principal loan, as opposed to applying the extra amount to the property taxes or property insurance.) The additional amounts paid by the borrower **do not** reduce *the monthly payments* for a conventional loan. Instead, the principal loan will be paid off sooner, reducing *the number of years* before the loan is paid in full. The benefit of a conventional loan is derived from the security of fixed monthly mortgage payments that it provides. The downside is that the applicant usually needs a fairly unblemished credit report in order to receive the most favorable interest rate, lowest points, etc.

FHA/VA Loans

Federal Housing Administration (FHA) and Department of Veterans Affairs (DVA) loans are backed by the federal government. The benefits include lower down-payment requirements and, in some cases, especially

A 15-YEAR MORTGAGE
VERSUS
A 30-YEAR MORTGAGE

Borrower A's 30-year mortgage after 5 years

Original mortgage amount	$50,000.00
Interest rate paid	12%
Monthly payment (principal + interest)	$ 514.31
Total amount paid over 5 years	$30,858.60
Total interest paid over 5 years	$29,689.90
Total principal paid over 5 years	$ 1,168.70
Mortgage balance after 5 years	$48,831.30

Borrower B's 15-year mortgage after 5 years

Original mortgage amount	$50,000.00
Interest rate paid	11½%
Monthly payment (principal + interest)	$ 584.09
Total amount paid over 5 years	$35,045.40
Total interest paid over 5 years	$26,590.21
Total principal paid over 5 years	$ 8,455.19
Mortgage balance after 5 years	$41,544.81

Figure 6-1.   A comparison between a 15-year and a 30-year mortgage after 5 years.

first-time buyers with good credit, the loans may be assumable with no prepayment penalty. The downside is that these types of loans may require more points (prepaid interest) than conventional loans and may have application red tape and delays in obtaining loan approvals.

Balloon Loans

Balloon loans offer the borrower lower rates and other flexible terms, especially when the loan is provided by the seller, but at the end of the mortgage term the entire remaining balance is still due in a *balloon*, or *lump-sum payment;* this requires the borrower to obtain new financing to pay off the loan.

Balloon loans are most commonly found in situations where the seller *holds the mortgage* (or *holds paper*), which means that the borrower (who is also the buyer in this case) makes payments to the seller each month instead of to a bank. This type of arrangement benefits the borrower who may be unable to obtain bank financing at this time because of insufficient provable income (i.e., a borrower who owns a cash business), or who has minor problems with his credit rating, not enough time at his current job, a recent bankruptcy, or a foreclosure. The borrower benefits by avoiding expensive closing costs such as points and origination fees that would have been charged by a lending institution if this was a traditional mortgage. Sellers benefit by attracting a wider range of buyers who don't want to wait several more years to own their own homes. At the end of the loan term (most commonly between one and five years), when the balloon payment for the remaining principal balance becomes due, the borrower is in a better position to obtain financing from another source, usually a lending institution. By this time the borrower has had a chance to show sufficient provable income on his or her tax return to qualify for a new mortgage loan, or to clear up the credit problems that prevented him or her from qualifying for a conventional loan. The borrower obtains the new financing, pays off the balance of the balloon loan to the seller, and makes future monthly mortgage payments to the new lender.

Some balloon terms require *interest-only payments*. This means that payments are only made for the contractual interest rate. The interest is paid to the seller on a monthly or quarterly basis, and at the end of the loan term, the borrower may have paid off all the interest on the loan, but still owes the original principal loan amount.

Balloon loans can be amortized over any period of time (i.e., 15, 20, 25, or 30-year terms). "Amortized" loans are those where the borrower's monthly payment will be allocated to both the principal loan and the interest, therefore, the monthly payments are for a larger amount than an interest-only loan.

Adjustable Rate Mortgages (ARMs)

Adjustable-rate (or variable-rate) mortgages (ARMs) are loans where the interest-rate changes on a prearranged payment schedule. The most common payment schedules are six-month, one-year, three-year, or five-year terms. On each anniversary date of the loan, the payments are adjusted according to the prevailing rate of interest. The benefit of this type of loan is that it generally offers lower initial rates than a fixed-rate loan, and it may be assumable by new buyers. Adjustable-rate loans also offer the possibility of future rate *decreases*, and may even be convertible to fixed-rate programs after a period of time that is contractually agreed to in the mortgage documents. The downside is that this type of loan carries the risk of interest rate increases, which would mean that monthly payments could increase significantly in future years if interest rates skyrocket.

Graduated-Payment Mortgages

Graduated-payment mortgages (GPMs) are loans in which the payment increases by preset amounts during the first few years and then stabilizes at a contractually agreed fixed interest rate. The difference between this type of loan and an ARM is that with a GPM loan you know in advance the percent that the interest rates will increase for the term of the loan, instead of having to rely on changeable market rates, as you do with an ARM.

The benefit of this type of mortgage is that it allows a borrower to begin paying the mortgage loan at a lower interest rate that he or she can afford now, with the understanding that the rates will go up gradually. This loan presumes that the periodic increases in the interest rates will be offset by the borrower's elevated salary level as his or her job-related experience leads to a higher earning capacity. The downside is that earning capacity may not increase as rapidly as anticipated, or that even if earnings increase, unexpected expenses (i.e., a baby) could cancel out (or exceed) the additional income that was earmarked to offset the higher mortgage payment.

Comparison Shopping for the Best Lender

There are two very important reasons for putting your time and effort into shopping for the mortgage loan that is right for you. *First,* you avoid wasting your time and money applying for a loan that does not suit your financial situation. *Second,* you avoid loans with inflated interest rates, and other overpriced costs associated with a mortgage loan.

Name of Lending Institution	Question #1	Question #2	Question #3	Question #4	Question #5	Question #6	Question #7	Question #8	etc.
ABC Bank									
DEF Bank									
XYZ Bank									
etc..									

Figure 6-2. A sample spreadsheet for comparing mortgage programs offered by lending institutions.

Begin by organizing your questions and answers onto a spreadsheet so that you can compare prices. To accomplish this, the method that I devised for myself (and still find to be the most effective way to comparison shop) can be completed in three-steps.

Step One: List the names of the lending institutions that you wish to contact on the left side of the spreadsheet. **Step Two:** Arrange the questions that you want to ask each lender across the top of the spreadsheet. (See Figure 6-2.) **Step Three**: Call each of the lenders on your list, ask them the questions from Step Two, and fill in the answers on your spreadsheet. When you are finished, you will have an organized overview of loan packages available, allowing you to compare each lender with its competitors, and assisting you in determining which lender has the best loan for you.

Key Questions to Ask a Lender

For Fixed and Adjustable Rate Loans, Ask the Following Questions:

How much is the bank attorney's fee? The bank attorney is hired by the lending institution and represents the lender's interests. The bank attorney reviews the loan application, the closing documents, the title reports, and confirms that the applicant and the loan terms are in compliance with the lender's guidelines. The applicant has little control over what the bank attorney charges. However, if the choices have been narrowed down to two lenders, both with the same rates and other terms, and one lender charges $250 for its bank attorney's fee, while the other lender charges $750, an applicant can either choose the lender with the lower fee or try to negotiate a lower price with the lender that is charging more. In any event, the differences in fees charged by bank attorneys that represent different banks may surprise you,.

How long must applicants be employed at their present jobs to qualify for a loan? Some lending institutions require loan applicants to be working for a certain length of time (commonly two years) at their present jobs. Some lenders are more flexible, and will take specific circumstances into consideration, such as a job transfers. What the lender *does not* want to see is a history of job-hopping or other inconsistent patterns of short-term employment that can interrupt the steady flow of income (income that the applicant needs to pay the mortgage).

Does the lender follow FNMA guidelines or portfolio its own loans? When banks lend mortgage money to borrowers, the borrowers sign a *note* (promising to repay the loan) and a *mortgage* (pledging the property as collateral for the loan). The mortgage instrument may be sold to the secondary market, if it meets the requisite guidelines, and the bank "recycles" the money from the sale of the mortgage into mortgage loans for the next applicants. The Federal National Mortgage Association—Fannie Mae— (introduced in Chapter 4 as a potential source of foreclosure listings) is the largest purchaser of mortgages in the secondary market. In order for lending institutions to sell mortgages to Fannie Mae, the loans must "conform to" the conditions that are clearly enumerated in "Fannie Mae Guidelines." There is a maximum mortgage amount that can be sold to Fannie Mae, and this maximum amount increases periodically. Loans that exceed the Fannie Mae limit are called "jumbo" loans. If a loan cannot be sold to Fannie Mae, the lender keeps the loan in its own portfolio. The lender's qualifying criteria for loans it keeps in its portfolio may be more lenient or more stringent than Fannie Mae's qualifying criteria. For example, a lender may require applicants to have a blemish-free credit rating for loans that it portfolios; another lender may be more concerned with the applicant's income-to-debt ratio (income minus expenses); and still another may prefer an applicant to have a higher loan-to-value ratio (more equity) in the property. Knowledge of lender's guidelines can be extremely valuable to foreclosure purchasers who are willing to do their homework. For instance, applicants can capitalize on their pristine credit by applying to a lender that rewards perfect credit ratings by offering much lower interest rates than its competitors are offering.

Can the interest rate of the loan be locked in? If you want to ensure that the interest rate you are quoted remains the same until the closing, you can ask for the rate to be *locked in.* Ask the lender how much it would cost for the lock-in and find out what would happen if the interest rates go down. Would you get the benefit of the lower rate? If not, the lock-in option may not be favorable because you could be penalized if you end up being locked into a higher rate.

What is the prevailing rate? The *prevailing rate* is the interest rate the lender is charging for the loan at the time of the quote. The prevailing rate can change daily.

How many points are being charged? A *point* is another name for *prepaid interest* and equals 1 percent of the mortgage loan (not the purchase price) that the applicant is applying for. For example, on a $150,000 mortgage loan, one point equals $1500.

Is there an origination fee, and how much is it? An *origination fee* is an administrative expense that many lenders charge as part of the loan cost. Lenders do not always charge an origination fee, nor are they required to. If the lender does charge an origination fee, the amount can range from $100 to several points.

How much is the application fee? The *application fee* is the amount a lender charges the borrower when it begins the application process. The application fee usually includes charges for a credit report, an appraisal of the property, and other fees. If the lender charges an application fee, ask if any part of the fee is refundable should the mortgage application be denied, or if the applicant does not accept the loan terms that the lender offers.

Is the mortgage assumable? Assumable loans are loans that are *taken over* by a purchaser who wishes to leave the existing mortgage loan intact. The purchaser pays the difference between the asking price and the mortgage balance in cash, and *assumes* the mortgage balance along with the responsibility for making future monthly payments to the lender. An assumable loan precludes the purchaser from having to qualify for a new mortgage from scratch, which in turn expedites the property transfer.

If the mortgage is assumable, find out what the procedure involves for someone to assume it. In some cases, the person who assumes the mortgage must be requalified by the lender (i.e., assumable *with bank permission*). In other cases, the lending institution will permit the purchaser to assume the mortgage by signing some papers (and sometimes paying a nominal administrative fee), and there are no other formalities.

Is there a prepayment penalty? A *prepayment penalty* is an extra charge to a borrower who pays off the mortgage balance before the end of the mortgage term, usually by refinancing, or by selling the property and paying off the loan in full. Federal laws may limit the amount that banks can charge for prepayment penalties.

Does the lender escrow for property taxes and property insurance? This means that the lender collects certain payments (most commonly property taxes and/or property insurance) each month as part of the mortgage payment. The lender holds the payment in an *escrow account*, or reserve fund, and when the payment is due, the lender forwards the taxes to the town or village and the insurance premiums to the insurance company. By controlling the monthly collection of the payments from the borrowers and its timely remittance to the creditors, the lender can protect its interests in the property. You will need to know how many months of escrow the lender will collect at the closing. The property tax and insurance escrows can be one of the more expensive closing costs. Federal laws limit the number of months of escrow reserves that lenders can require borrowers to pay in advance.

How many months of assets (i.e., cash) does the lender require applicants to have available in their bank accounts for the loan to close? Some lenders require applicants to have enough money to cover one or two months of mortgage payments (including property taxes and property insurance if the bank is escrowing for those expenses) in the event that an emergency interrupts the applicant's income.

Does the lender require "seasoning" before approving a loan? Some lenders require an applicant who wishes to obtain a mortgage on a home that he or she already owns, to have owned that home for one or two years (a.k.a. "seasoning") before applying for a mortgage loan or a refinance.

Will the lender consider the credit limits on the applicant's credit cards as debt? In calculating the applicant's income-to-debt ratio, lenders look at the credit lines on the applicant's credit cards. Even though the applicant pays the balance in full each month and has no outstanding balance due, some lenders take into account the possibility that the applicant could, at any time, go out and borrow up to the limit on all of the credit cards. If it is the lender's policy to consider the applicant's maximum limits as debt even when there is no outstanding balance, someone who is in this situation and applies for a loan with that lender may be wasting his or her time and/or money for the application fee. In some cases, the situation can easily be remedied if the applicant closes out the credit card accounts and/or lowers the limits on the lines of credit _before_ applying for a loan. Another alternative is for the applicant to select a lender that only considers the outstanding credit card balances in calculating the income-to debt ratios.

For Adjustable Rate Loans Only (ARMs)
Ask the Following Questions:

What index does the lender use? The index is the bank's rate of borrowing, or the amount that the lender is charged to put money out on the street to borrowers. All lenders use one specific index, which is specified within the mortgage documents. The current rate of that index can be found in most local newspapers. Interest rates on ARMs adjust according to the average of the index.

What is the lender's margin? The lender's margin is the percent of profit a bank wants to make above the index. This amount remains the same over the term of the mortgage. It is calculated as follows:

> Index + Margin = Prevailing Rate of Interest

If the rate of borrowing (index) is 7 percent and the margin (profit) is 2 percent, the rate that is quoted is 9 percent.

When are the rates adjusted? The most common adjustment periods are six months, one year, and three years. This means that interest rates, and, as a result, the monthly mortgage amount, will be adjusted every six-month, one-year, or three-year anniversary.

What is the term cap? The *term cap* is the maximum amount that the interest rates can go up or down during each adjustment period.

What is the life cap? The *life cap* is the maximum amount the interest rates can go up or down during the life of the loan. For example, on a 30-year mortgage with a life cap of 16 percent, the interest rate may fluctuate up to or below that amount, but may *never* exceed it.

What year does the lender use as a basis for qualifying an applicant? When calculating an applicant's qualifying ratios for an adjustable-rate mortgage, lenders frequently do so using the maximum anticipated increase (up to the term cap) on the loan's first anniversary.

Thus, an applicant who wants a one-year ARM, with a 2-percent term cap, and who is locked in at a 6-percent interest rate for the first year, will most likely be qualified based on the maximum rate the loan could adjust to on its first anniversary: 6-percent initial rate + 2-percent maximum term cap = 8 percent.

Is the mortgage convertible to a fixed-rate loan, and what is the procedure? Adjustable loans with a convertible feature are popular because they allow applicants to start off with the lower initial interest rate of the adjustable loan, and then give them the option of converting to a fixed-rate loan later on. The procedures to follow and the costs involved with the fixed-rate conversion are included in the loan documents. Some lenders allow the applicant to convert the loan to a fixed rate after the first year by paying a small administrative fee, and other lenders require the applicant to wait for several years before the conversion feature becomes available.

Is the loan negatively amortized? Normally, homeowners expect to reduce the principal balance of the amount they borrowed by making their monthly mortgage payments. However, when the prevailing rate (index + margin) exceeds the maximum term cap allowed, the extra cost is passed along to the borrower if the loan is negatively amortized, and the mortgage balance can *increase* instead of growing *smaller* as time goes on.

As an example, assume we have a loan with a 9-percent interest rate and a 1-percent term cap. For the period prior to its 1-year anniversary, the index on the loan averaged a 2-percent interest rate increase. The new interest rate should be 11 percent, but because of the 1-percent term cap, the maximum interest rate increase is to 10 percent.

In a regularly amortizing loan, the lender would absorb the 1-percent difference between the 11 percent the borrower should have been paying, and the 10 percent he is capped at. *In a negatively amortizing loan,* however, the lender can require the borrower to remit payment for the negative difference before the new loan period begins, or the lender will add the amount to the borrower's mortgage balance. If the amount is added to the mortgage balance, when the new monthly payments are calculated, the borrower's payments will be based on the increased mortgage balance.

In this chapter, we covered the most popular forms of *traditional* financing that are available for foreclosure purchasers. Those who wish to pursue more *creative* approaches to financing foreclosures will find them in Chapter 7.

7

Creative Alternatives for Financing Foreclosures

A majority of purchasers finance foreclosures with traditional mortgage loans. Whether you have a lot of cash, very little cash, good credit, or "not so good" credit, there are a number of creative strategies that can be implemented in conjunction with, or as a replacement for, traditional mortgage financing. Chapter 7 provides examples of these initiatives for the four categories of foreclosure purchasers:

Category #1–Foreclosure Purchasers with Limited Cash and Good Credit

Category #2–Foreclosure Purchasers with Limited Cash and Tarnished Credit

Category #3–Foreclosure Purchasers with A Lot of Cash and Good Credit

Category #4–Foreclosure Purchasers with A Lot of Cash and Tarnished Credit

CATEGORY #1—Foreclosure Purchasers with Limited Cash and Good Credit

People in Category #1 who wish to purchase foreclosures should consider these alternatives:

Put the Equity in Your Home to Good Use

If you currently own a home and have lived there for a number of years, the equity* you have accumulated can be a valuable resource to tap for financing another property. Let's say that 10 years ago, you purchased a handyman's special for $100,000, put $10,000 down as a down payment, and took out a mortgage loan to finance the remaining $90,000. Depending on how much the property values have appreciated in your area, and especially if you have made improvements to the premises, the value of your home may have increased substantially during the time you've owned it.

If the house is your primary dwelling, you can refinance the existing mortgage or, if you paid off the mortgage, you can apply for a new one. (An investment property may be more difficult to refinance.) Another

---

* The **equity** in your home is calculated by subtracting the remaining mortgage balance from the current market value.

REFINANCING A 10-YEAR OLD MORTGAGE

Purchase price $100,000

Down payment $–10,000

Mortgage amount $ 90,000 (30 years at 10% interest)

Current value $150,000

Refinance amount $120,000 (80% of current value)

Note: To calculate the amount of cash available, you deduct the remaining mortgage balance from the (above) refinance amount.

Figure 7-1. Refinancing a 10-year-old mortgage.

TAKING AN EQUITY LOAN OR 2D MORTGAGE

Purchase price $100,000

Down payment $–10,000

Mortgage loan amount $ 90,000

Current value $150,000

Refinance amount $105,000 *(70% of current value)*

Note: To calculate the amount of cash available, you deduct the remaining mortgage balance from the (above) refinance amount.

Figure 7-2. Taking out an equity loan or a second mortgage.

option is to apply for an equity loan or a second mortgage, and use the proceeds to purchase your foreclosure. Figure 7-1 illustrates the refinancing option and Figure 7-2 illustrates the equity loan or second mortgage option.

The benefit of tapping into the equity in your present home is that you keep the property you have and you use that equity to buy more real estate, which will appreciate over time. Whether you rent the premises to a tenant, whose monthly rent payment covers all or most of the monthly amount of your new loan, or you fix up and sell the foreclosure for a profit and pay off the loan, you have used your money to buy another appreciable asset and, consequently, to increase your wealth.

Obtain Financing from Banks and Government Agencies to Purchase (REO) Foreclosures from Their Inventories

If you have decided to buy a bank-owned foreclosure from a lending institution's inventory (a.k.a. an REO), or a government-owned foreclosure that has been repossessed by an agency such as HUD, the DVA, the FDIC, or the GSA, you should know that the bank or government agency has the authority and the motivation to offer extremely favorable financing terms on mortgage loans for properties in their inventories. As I mentioned in Chapters 3 and 4, lending institutions and government agencies *are not* in the business of managing and selling real estate. They would much rather provide financing so that people can buy the properties, than to keep the properties in their inventories where it costs them a lot of money to maintain. The benefits of obtaining financing from banks and government agencies includes discounts on interest rates and closing costs, lower down payment requirements, etc.

Obtain Financing from A Foreclosing Lender before a Property Is Auctioned

In some cases, when a loan is in default, the foreclosing lender agrees to allow a purchaser to assume the loan balance before the property goes to auction (see Chapter 5). The foreclosing lender may even agree to waive some of the late charges and back payments that have recently accrued. It is clearly more advantageous for a lender to substitute a new borrower who is financially capable of paying the monthly payments, and who is willing to assume the delinquent owner's loan. The benefit to the purchaser is the possibility of homeownership by assuming the mortgage loan balance with little or no cash outlay. The downside is the expense of applying for a new loan if the foreclosing lender requires the purchaser to get his or her own new financing instead of allowing the existing loan to be assumed.

Get Your Foot in the Door with a
Hard-Money Loan

Another option for financing a foreclosure is a *hard-money loan*. This is *not* "break-your-arm" financing from a loan shark. Rather, it is a financing tool that is driven by the equity in the property, rather than the borrower's good credit rating. The benefit of this type of loan is its availability to applicants within a few days. It is, therefore, very desirable when fast cash is needed. The drawbacks are the high points and high interest rates charged. Consequently, this form of financing is **only** recommended for a **short** period of time. You should replace it as soon as possible with a mortgage loan bearing a lower interest rate.

Build Wealth through
Contract Transfers

Another way that people can build up enough money to purchase a foreclosure is through profits on contract transfers. In many cases, the sales contract issued to the high bidder at the auction is assignable (transferable), unless there is language in the contract that expressly forbids assignment. Since the successful bidder is expected to come up with cash for the purchase, the sale is not contingent upon the buyer's ability to secure financing. Therefore, the contract can be transferred to a new buyer, as long as the new buyer has the money required to close. People have made a lucrative business out of successfully bidding on properties at auctions and then assigning them to other buyers before the closing. The new buyer refunds the original bidder's down payment plus an agreed-upon profit, and becomes the new contract vendee.

As illustrated in Figure 7-3, let's assume you are bidding on a property that is worth $125,000. You purchase it at the auction for $75,000. You give the referee $7500 as the 10 percent down payment. There is $67,500 due at closing. You assign the contract to a new buyer and the new buyer pays you a down payment of $12,500, which is a reimbursement of your $7500 down payment plus a (totally negotiable) profit of $5000. The new buyer closes with $67,500 still due from your original contract. The benefit to the new buyer is buying a $125,000 property for $80,000. You earned a quick $5000 for bidding and assigning the contract to someone else.

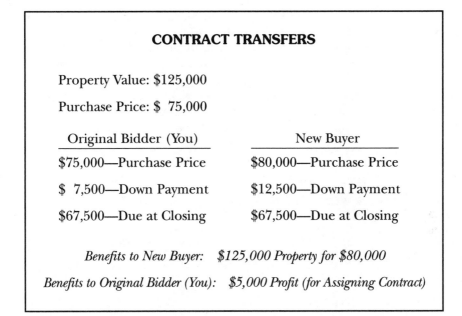

CONTRACT TRANSFERS

Property Value: $125,000

Purchase Price: $ 75,000

Original Bidder (You)	New Buyer
$75,000—Purchase Price	$80,000—Purchase Price
$ 7,500—Down Payment	$12,500—Down Payment
$67,500—Due at Closing	$67,500—Due at Closing

Benefits to New Buyer: $125,000 Property for $80,000

Benefits to Original Bidder (You): $5,000 Profit (for Assigning Contract)

Figure 7-3. A contract transfer.

It is important to remember that this technique only works for cash purchases. When there is financing involved from the foreclosing lender (i.e., you purchase an REO and the bank that owns the property agrees to give you financing) then the loan will be contingent upon **your** credit history and income, and usually **_will not_** be assignable.

The downside risk in contract transfer arrangements can be significant. You must be certain that the new buyer to whom you assigned your contract is financially able to come up with the cash for the closing. If the new buyer is not able to close, you may still be contractually required to complete the transaction as the original contract vendee, and if you are unable to do so, you risk forfeiting your down payment. Additional penalties may be also be imposed pursuant to the "terms of sale" (as discussed in Chapter 3—"No Down Payment Refunds").

Borrow Against Whole Life Insurance Policies—(Are You Sitting on Hidden Treasure?)

Have you owned a whole life insurance policy for a number of years? If so, then chances are you've accumulated a good amount of cash in that policy by now and you may have some options to consider.

You can use the cash in your policy to buy a foreclosure. Or you can borrow money from a bank using the cash in your policy as collateral and assign the ownership of the policy to the bank. Finally, you can take out a loan from a bank based on the policy's cash value. Using the cash you have accumulated in your policy as collateral, you can repay the loan and pay a fraction of the interest rate you would have paid on a typical personal or mortgage loan. Contact your insurance agent to discuss the viability of this financing alternative in your particular circumstances.

Category #2—Foreclosure Purchasers with Limited Cash and Tarnished Credit

People in Category #2 who wish to purchase foreclosures should consider these alternatives:

Buy Foreclosures with Partners

It has become increasingly popular for people to purchase foreclosures with partners. There are many wealthy professionals out there with great credit ratings and lots of cash, but with no time to do the legwork that plays an essential role in any foreclosure purchase. If your funds are limited but you have the time and the knowledge to acquire foreclosures, then you can offer those services as your contribution to the partnership.

People in Category #2 need to build up their credit and their finances which is a slow process. For those of you without enough cash to go out and buy a foreclosure, partnerships are an ideal way to help you accomplish your goals even when you are not yet able to do so independently. With each new venture, the profits that you earn will continue to accumulate until eventually, you will find yourself in a position where you have enough money to purchase a foreclosure without partners.

There are many benefits to all parties that can be derived from this type of arrangement, including the pooling of expertise and financial backing, the ability to share expenses, and, if you are new at this endeavor, the security of having the support of partners who share the same interest as you. The downside is that this partnership usually involves a sharing of control, which could lead to many disagreements unless each partner's role is clearly defined in a written agreement.

An overview of partnership functions and roles. Partnerships formed for the purpose of purchasing foreclosures may be organized in several ways.

The "cash" contributor's function is to provide the money with which the partnership will purchase (and repair) the property.

The "time and legwork" contributor's function is most likely to locate a foreclosure and provide documented evidence for the other partner(s) that the property is a good investment. These preliminary preparations are covered in greater detail in Chapter 9. Other duties for the time and legwork partner might include providing an analysis of the property's current market value prior to repairs, calculating the anticipated purchase price, obtaining estimates for the costs and time to complete the repairs (see Chapter 13 for more details about hiring a contractor), and estimating the anticipated sales price after repairs are completed, and the profit split after the property is sold. An example of how such a partnership arrangement would look on paper is illustrated in Figure 7-4.

Variations of partnerships. Unlike traditional contracts between buyers and sellers, when partnerships are formed for the purpose of buying foreclosures, the relationship usually survives beyond the date of the purchase.

Three equal partners. Figure 7-5 illustrates a variation where three people with equal cash contributions of $25,000 get together to purchase a property at an auction for $75,000 cash. They each put an additional $5,000 into repairs, and then sell the property for $150,000 one month later. In this case, the total individual contribution of $30,000 makes each partner $50,000, or a profit of $20,000 (a 66.6-percent return on their investment). Not bad for one month's work!

Other partnership options. You will need to decide whether you are interested in a long-term partnership—where you and your partners rent out the property to tenants for an agreed period of time before you sell it—or a short-term partnership—where you and your partners fix up and resell the property for a profit soon after you purchase it. Another partnership option could be to allow one of the partners to refinance and buy out the other partners. Equity sharing (see Chapter 8) is yet another form of a partnership—one that pairs owner-occupants with investors.

Foreclosure purchasers who wish to form partnerships to help finance their foreclosures are strongly advised to seek the advice of financial advisors, and to hire an attorney who is experienced in real estate partnerships to prepare an agreement that clearly defines each partner's duties, roles, intentions, goals, etc.

Category #3—Foreclosure Purchasers with a Lot of Cash and Good Credit

People in Category #3 who wish to purchase foreclosures should consider these alternatives:

BUYING WITH PARTNERS—ORGANIZER PLUS THREE CASH CONTRIBUTORS

☐ The Roles of Four Partners

Partner 1:

Role:	Organizer
Contribution:	Expertise, Legwork; No Cash Investment

Partners 2, 3, & 4:

Role:	Financial
Contribution:	$ 30,000 Cash Each
Breakdown:	$ 25,000 Each Toward Purchase Price
	$ 5,000 Each Toward Repair Costs
Total Cash Outlay:	$ 90,000

☐ Foreclosure Purchase—Cost Analysis

Purchase Price	$ 75,000
Add: Repairs Cost	$ 15,000
Total Costs	$ 90,000

The Four Partners Sell the Property One Month After Its Purchase. During This Time, All Necessary Repairs Have Been Made.

☐ Foreclosure Sale—Profit Analysis

Sales Price	$150,000
Each Partner's Split	$ 37,500 Each (4 Equal Shares)

Partner 1: (Organizer) $ 37,500 Profit

Partner 2, 3, 4: (Financial) $ 7,500 Profit (25% Return on Investment)

Figure 7-4. A sample partnership arrangement.

BUYING WITH PARTNERS—THREE
EQUAL CASH CONTRIBUTORS

☐ Partners 1, 2, and 3

Role: Financial

Contribution: $ 30,000 Cash Each

Total Cash Outlay: $ 90,000

☐ Foreclosure Purchase—Cost Analysis

Purchase Price: $ 75,000

Repairs: $ 15,000

Total Cost: $ 90,000

☐ Foreclosure Sale—Profit Analysis

Sales Price: $150,000

Each Partner's Split: $ 50,000 Each (3 Equal Shares)

Partners 1, 2, and 3 **$ 20,000 Profit (66.6%**

Return on Investment)

Figure 7-5. Sample partnership arrangement—three equal partners.

All of the Above Plus...

If you have cash and good credit, you have the advantage of being able to purchase foreclosures with any of the aforementioned strategies recommended to the people in Category #1 and Category #2. Your access to cash and credit also provides you with some additional creative options.

Buy Foreclosures with Cash at the Auction

You can purchase foreclosures with cash, fix them up, and flip (sell) them to someone else for a profit. Or if you want to keep the property as an investment and rent it out to tenants, you can purchase the property at the auction with cash, fix it up, and obtain financing from a bank later. Your advantage is in having the financial resources to keep the property while it builds equity. The downside is that if you don't do your "homework" and purchase a property safely and sanely, it can cost you money instead of making you money.

Buy Foreclosures in Bulk from Banks and Government Agencies

You can also use your resources of cash and credit to your advantage if you buy more than one property at a time. You can offer to pay cash as a down payment on several properties, while the bank or government agency will provide financing for the balance due. The benefit is that you can get discounts on the prices of the properties when purchasing them in bulk. The downside is the expense of the closing costs for multiple properties. But this cost can be offset by taking one *blanket mortgage* on all properties and incorporating a "release clause" into the mortgage terms for any property that you sell off. Here is an example of how it works:

You purchase four properties for $600,000, put down $100,000 as a down payment and get a mortgage for the remaining $500,000. You allocate the mortgage for the four properties in accordance with their values. In this example, all four properties have similar values and the purchase prices will be allocated equally at $150,000. The down payment of $100,000 is also allocated equally, $25,000 to each property. The remaining balance of $125,000 for each of the four properties is financed through the bank, but instead of four different mortgages and four separate closings and costs, you have one blanket mortgage for $500,000 (one closing) with a release clause that requires a payment of $125,000 to the lender for each property that is sold. This means that instead of the entire mortgage coming due if one property is sold, each property can be sold off independently, and the blanket mortgage remains intact for the rest of the loans. So in two years, if you sell one of the properties for $200,000, you pay off the "release" amount that was allocated in the amount of $125,000 to the bank, and the remaining $75,000 is your profit. The new mortgage balance remaining on the loan is reduced by the $125,000 you have just paid off. The remaining mortgage balance of $375,000 (less the monthly mortgage payments you have been paying) will be reduced further each time another property is sold off.

Category #4—Foreclosure Purchasers with a Lot of Cash and Tarnished Credit

People in Category #4 who wish to purchase foreclosures should consider these alternatives:

Purchase Now and Finance Later

You can use your cash to help you reestablish credit. If a lender will give you financing, but it would be expensive, you may be able to reduce the costs by purchasing with a partner who has good credit. This way, you can at least obtain financing initially. As your payments are made in a timely fashion, you continue to repair your credit, until you can eventually qualify for financing on your own. You can arrange in advance to either buy out your partner if you really want to keep the property, or you can sell the property and use your share of the proceeds as a down payment on a different property.

Depending on the reason for the tarnished credit, a purchaser in Category 4 may encounter difficulty obtaining a loan, and may end up paying a very high interest rate and several points in order for a loan to be approved. While the increased loan costs are understandable in order for you to obtain the loan, one option is to find a lender that will agree—in writing—to renegotiate a lower rate of interest after you have proven yourself by making timely payments for a pre-agreed period of time.

If you are unable to find a lender to finance property for you, another option is to buy the foreclosure with cash and obtain financing down the road, after you have reestablished credit in other ways (i.e., a secured credit card). Consult a credit counselor who can help you define a plan of action to repair your credit in a time frame that is compatible with your investing goals.

8

Equity Sharing: Buying Foreclosures with a Partner

Equity sharing is a creative approach to buying foreclosures with a partner, sharing the benefits derived from that partnership during the term of the agreement, and splitting the profits after the property is sold and the partnership term ends.

In Chapter 8, we revisit the partnership concept from Chapter 7 and apply it in two circumstances where equity sharing strongly benefits the participants. The first arrangement is between parents and children; the second arrangement is between investors and contractors.

How It Works

An equity-sharing arrangement involves two partners. One partner is the *inside occupant*; the other partner is the *outside investor*. The inside occupant lives in the house and generally contributes less money towards purchasing and financing the premises and more towards the monthly expenses. The outside investor does not live in the house and generally contributes less money towards the monthly expenses, and more towards purchasing and financing the property.

For the purposes of the equity-sharing arrangements that are discussed in this chapter, each of the partners owns a 50-percent interest in the property and both partners have their names on the mortgage, note, and deed.

Equity sharing is based on the premise that real estate will appreciate in value over time. It is implemented *most effectively* in a rising real estate market.

Why It Works

In order to appreciate fully the benefits that equity sharing brings to those involved, we must first understand each party's goals and the challenges they face in trying to achieve them.

The Owner-Occupant's Goals and Challenges

The Goals

The two main objectives for homebuyers are first, to attain *"the American Dream of Homeownership"* for their families to live in for many years to come and second, to finance their *"American Dream"* with a mortgage loan that the buyers can afford to pay on time every month.

The Challenges

High Housing Costs Make Ownership an Illusion   In today's residential real estate market, high interest rates and costly housing prices can cause the *"American Dream of Homeownership"* to remain an elusive fantasy for many people. In addition, escalating rental prices preclude many tenants from saving enough money to buy their own homes. Traditionally, a buyer needs enough cash for a 10-percent down-payment, and, depending on the financing practices in the state where the property is located, anywhere from 5 percent to 10 percent of the mortgage amount for closing costs. When people without substantial financial resources strive to acquire a home of their own, these challenges often appear to be insurmountable.

The Investor's Goals and Challenges

The Goals

In order to address the problems faced by today's real estate investors, we must understand their main objectives. An investor is someone who purchases real estate at a below-market price, without any intention of occupying it as a primary dwelling, using as little of his (or her) own money as possible. Investment property can be "income-producing" (where the "income produced' is the monthly rental amount paid by the tenant to the landlord), and "nonincome-producing" (where no income is produced, but the property is occupied by the investor, on a very limited basis, as a second home and/or a vacation home). An investor typically holds onto income-producing property for a number of years and rents it out to tenants during that time. Consequently, the investor maintains ownership of the property, and the tenant pays a monthly rent payment that covers most, if not all, of the investor's monthly mortgage payment. The investor benefits because the rent income is used to pay the monthly mortgage, which, in turn, reduces the balance of the outstanding mortgage loan, and builds equity for the investor. With careful planning, at some point in the future the property will be sold, and the proceeds will provide a source of liquid funds to help finance the investor's retirement. There are, however, certain aspects of owning income-producing rental property that can be financially troubling for inexperienced landlords.

The Challenges

Problems with Tenants   When investors rent out property to others, they become landlords. Problems can arise if the investors do not take their responsibilities as landlords seriously. The most common problem that investors encounter is when tenants violate their lease agreements. Being a landlord requires much more than just collecting the rent and paying the mortgage each month. Typical headaches for landlords include:

Vacancies.   The mortgage payment comes out of the landlord's pocket if there are no tenants living in the property and paying the rent.

Repair costs.   Inexperienced landlords may have a lease that does not protect them properly when disputes arise with their tenants.

Tenant turnover.   Depending on the length of tenancy specified in the lease, there may be a yearly turnover of tenants, which may require a new paint job, interior and exterior cleaning, and costly advertising expenses.

Rent collection.   Your tenants may have a problem paying their rent on time—or at all!

Deadbeat tenants.   Unless a landlord is experienced in screening prospective tenants, he or she runs the risk of renting to a "deadbeat" tenant who refuses to pay the rent and who damages the rental property.

Problems with the High Cost of Loans for Investors

High interest rates.   From a mortgage lender's standpoint, there are two classifications of property owners: owner-occupants who use the property as their primary dwelling, and investors who use the premises as a rental property or a vacation home. Interest rates for investor loans are almost always higher than interest rates for owner-occupant loans because there is a greater risk factor involved. Why? When an applicant applies for a mortgage loan on a property he or she will be living in, the lender's qualifying process ensures that the applicant who will be occupying the premises has the financial capability to repay the loan each month. On the other hand, when an investor purchases a property to rent out to tenants, the lender's qualifying process only extends to the investor, not to the tenants who will be occupying the premises, and the lender has no control over the manner in which the investor qualifies the tenants. Although many lenders take the anticipated rental income (or a percent thereof) into consideration when calculating the investor's income to debt ratio during the qualification process, if the investor leases the property to tenants who do not pay their rent, and the investor is unable to carry the mortgage without that rental income, the mortgage on the rental property could end up in default. Thus, banks offset the investor's greater risk of default by charging higher interest rates and more points for mortgage loans on investment properties, and this, in turn, increases the monthly expenses and, in many cases, eliminates the expectation of a positive cash flow.

Negative cash flow. Cash flow is the money that "flows" into and out of a rental property. A *positive cash flow* is achieved when the income flowing into the property exceeds the expenditures flowing out of the property. A *negative cash flow* results when expenditures exceed income.

For example, let's say that we are looking for a foreclosure to purchase as an investment property, and intend to rent it out to tenants. As part of our preliminary preparations, we perform a cash flow analysis (see Chapter 9 - *Calculating Cash Flow*). We subtract the carrying charges and expenses flowing out of the property (i.e., mortgage payment, property taxes, property insurance) here, totaling $1550 per month from the rental income of $1500 per month flowing into the property, and we can project a negative cash flow of approximately $50 per month.

Monthly rent income:	$1,500.00 per month
Monthly expenses:	(1,550.00) per month
Negative cash flow:	($ 50.00) per month

A 25-percent down payment requirement. Another big headache for investors is the 25-percent down payment lender's require for a mortgage loan approval. By contrast, the owner-occupant can get financing with as little as 5 percent to 10 percent down (and even less with some government-backed loans). Once again, this is tied to the greater risk factor for loans on investor rental properties. Remember...investors do not like to use their own money, and the substantially higher cash outlay they are required to make is particularly irritating.

Owner-Occupants versus Investors—Comparing Purchases

Figure 8-1 illustrates the differences in the purchasing and in the financing costs when owner occupants buy property to live in and when investors buy property to rent out to tenants. The facts for both purchases are as follows:

COMPARING PURCHASES
OWNER-OCCUPANT VERSUS INVESTOR

Purchase price: $100,000

Yearly property taxes: $ 2,000

Projected rental income monthly: $ 800

	As Owner-Occupant	**As Investor**
Mortgage loan:		
Interest rate (%)	10%	10½%
Yearly earnings needed	$ 45,000	$ 40,000
Purchase price	$100,000	$100,000
Less: Down payment	(10,000)—10%	(25,000)—25%
Mortgage loan needed	$ 90,000	$ 75,000
Cash required:		
Down payment	$ 10,000	$ 25,000
Add: closing costs (10%)	$ 9,000	$ 7,500
Total cash needed	$ 19,000	$ 32,500
Monthly mortgage costs:		
Mortgage information	$ 90,000/30 yr.	$ 75,000/30 yr
Interest Rate	10%	10½%
Principal and interest	$ 789.82	$ 686.06
Property taxes	$ 167.00	$ 167.00
Property insurance	$ 50.00	$ 50.00
PMI	$ 25.00	
Monthly mortgage payment	$1,031.82	$ 903.06
Monthly cash flow:		
Rental income		$ 800.00
Less: Carrying		(903.06)
Monthly cash flow		$(103.06)

Figure 8-1.   Owner-occupant versus investor—comparing purchases.

The subject property in Figure 8-1 is being purchased for $100,000. The yearly property taxes are $2000 and the projected rental income is $800 per month. The monthly mortgage payment includes the mortgage principal and interest, and the loan will be fully amortized over 30 years.

Interest Rate

In this owner-occupant versus investor situation, we have an owner-occupant who is paying a 10 percent interest rate, compared to an investor who is paying the higher rate of 10½ percent. *Advantage: Owner-occupant*

Earnings

Because he is required to put a lower percent down, and therefore, requires a larger mortgage loan, the owner-occupant needs an annual income of approximately $45,000 compared to the investor who only needs $40,000 in earnings. *Advantage: Investor*

Down Payment

The owner-occupant is traditionally required to put a lower down payment (only 10 percent compared to 25 percent for the investor). *Advantage: Owner-occupant*

Closing Costs

The closing costs in Figure 8-1 include the owner-occupant's attorney fees, escrow charges for taxes and insurance, title fees, appraisal fees, and the bank attorney fees, as well as other ordinary closing costs. Closing costs vary from state to state, but in this example the 10-percent applied to both the owner-occupant and the investor.

The owner-occupant needs a total of $19,000 to complete the transaction. This includes the 10-percent down payment of $10,000 plus closing costs of $9000 (estimated as 10-percent of the $90,000 mortgage). The investor needs a total of $32,500 for this transaction. This amount includes the 25 percent down payment of $25,000 plus closing costs of $7500 (estimated at 10 percent of the $75,000 mortgage). *Advantage: Owner-occupant*

Monthly Mortgage Payment

The owner-occupant's monthly payment will also initially include private mortgage insurance (PMI) costs of approximately $25 per month since the purchaser is putting down less than 25 percent to purchase the property. The total monthly cost to the owner-occupant is $1031.82. *Advantage: Investor*

Summary of Costs for the Owner-Occupant

The owner-occupant will pay a lower interest rate than the investor, but must pay an additional amount each month to cover the private mortgage insurance. The owner-occupant must save the formidable sum of $19,000 for the down payment and closing costs, and show income of at least $45,000 to qualify for a $90,000 mortgage loan.

Summary of Costs for the Investor

The investor will pay a higher interest rate than the owner-occupant, but will not have to pay private mortgage insurance because of his 25-percent down payment. The investor must come up with $32,500 for the down payment and closing costs, and show income of at least $40,000.

So What Do We Have?

We have an owner-occupant who must try to save $19,000 and hope that by the time he does, housing costs will not have increased beyond his price range. We have an investor who does not want to use his own cash, but who, nevertheless, must come up with more money than the owner-occupant, and, to add insult to injury, the investor will suffer a negative cash flow in excess of $100 a month!

Equity Sharing to the Rescue

Equity sharing eliminates many of the aforementioned problems faced by homebuyers and investors. When two individuals buy a property as co-owners under an equity sharing agreement, they *each* get the best of both worlds. How? By seamlessly bridging the gap between the investor's need for "*affordable financing*" and the owner-occupant's quest for "*affordable housing.*"

The Inside Occupant

The inside occupant (we'll call this partner the "insider") can now achieve home ownership for a much smaller cash outlay than if he or she purchased the property individually.

The Outside Investor

The outside occupant (we'll call this partner the "investor") can still retain his income tax benefits, but loses the "high risk" stigma that caused the "high loan" costs. Also tenant problems and overall risk are minimal when the tenant is also an owner.

As illustrated in Figure 8-2, each partner gets the benefit of the other partner's advantages while eliminating the terms that had been so problematic. A new, favorable financial picture begins to emerge:

Interest Rate

The investor now shares the benefit of the lower interest rate previously available only to the owner-occupant (10 percent instead of 10½ percent) since his partner (the insider) <u>will</u> live in the house.

Earnings

The insider does not have to earn as much income to qualify for the loan, because the investor is now a co-borrower, and his or her income is combined with the insider's during the income qualifying process.

Down Payment

The investor gets the benefit of the insider's lower down payment requirement—10 percent instead of 25 percent—because this purchase is no longer considered an investment. Since one of the partners (the insider) will be living in the house, equity sharing gives both partners the insider's "owner-occupant" status. Remember, investors like to use as little of their own money as possible!

Negative Cash Flow

Negative cash flow for the investor is eliminated since the insider's "rent" each month will pay the carrying charges on the property.

Contract Terms to Agree Upon

As I said earlier, the beauty of equity-sharing arrangements is in the flexibility of the terms of the agreement. Each party should consult with an attorney, an accountant and/or a financial advisor to ensure that

EQUITY SHARING ARRANGEMENT—90/10 SPLIT

Purchase price:	$100,000
Down payment required:	$ 10,000 (*10% of purchase price*)
Mortgage needed:	$ 90,000
Closing costs needed:	$ 9,000 (*10% of mortgage needs*)

	Investor*	Insider*
Down payment contribution	$ 9,000	$1,000
Closing cost contribution	+ 8,100	+ 900
Total cash contribution required	$ 17,100	$1,900

*Investor contributes 90% and insider contributes 10% of the down payment and closing costs.

Figure 8-2. A 90-percent/10-percent split under an equity-sharing arrangement.

each partner's needs are provided for. The following are some of the terms to consider.

The Purchase Price Limits

The price of the property to be purchased in the venture must be determined and agreed to initially by both the insider and the investor, since both partners will be co-owners.

The Percent of Down Payment and Closing Cost Contributions

The insider and the investor must agree to the portion of the down payment and closing costs that each party will contribute. In some cases, the investor agrees to pay the entire down payment and closing costs, and in other cases, the partners agree to a 50-50 split in which each partner pays 50 percent of the amounts needed. Also commonly used is a 60-40 split in which the investor pays 60 percent of the down payment and closing costs, and the insider pays 40 percent. A 70-30 split, an 80-20 split, and a 90-10 split are also common arrangements.

Figure 8-2 illustrates a 90/10 split in which the investor contributes 90 percent of the down payment and closing costs and the insider contributes 10 percent. The purchase price is set at $100,000, and a 10-percent down payment $10,000 is required. Total closing costs are estimated at 10-percent of the mortgage amount of $90,000, or $9000. The total down payment and closing costs for both partners to split is $19,000. In this example of a 90/10 split, the investor will pay 90 percent of $19,000, which amounts to $17,100, and the insider will pay 10 percent of $19,000, which amounts to $1,900. Now, compare these numbers to the total amount each would have had to pay without equity sharing: the investor's required cash outlay plummeted from $32,500 to $17,100 and the insider's cash outlay fell from $19,000 to $1,900.

The agreed-upon contribution does not have to be the same percent for the down payment and the closing costs. For instance, the agreement may call for a 90/10 split towards the down payment, but each will contribute equally (a 50/50 split) towards the closing costs.

The Contribution for the Monthly Carrying Charges

In some cases the partners agree that the carrying charges (mortgage payment of principal, interest, property taxes, and property insurance) will be treated as the insider's monthly rent. This means that the insider will pay the total monthly mortgage costs for the property. Again, there are no hard and fast rules about the way the carrying charges are split. It may be agreed that the insider and investor will share the carrying charges equally. Internal Revenue Service regulations may require that the insider pay what would be considered fair market "rent" to the investor for using the half of the house that the investor owns, since technically both partners own the property and the insider is occupying both his or her half plus the investor's half.

For example, let's say two partners buy a property for $100,000. They put $10,000 down, and borrow $90,000. The loan is amortized over 30 years at a 10-percent interest rate. The monthly mortgage payment for principal and interest is $789.82 (round up to $790). In a typical arrangement, the insider would write a check to the mortgage lender for $395, which is half of the $790 mortgage payment. The investor would write a check for the other half. In addition, the insider would write another check for $395 payable to the investor to reflect the amount due as rent for the half of the home that the investor owns but the insider occupies. In such a case, investors may be required to report the amount paid to them by insiders (for the use of their half of the property) as rental income. In some cases the IRS may disallow some of the income tax deductions taken by either party unless "fair market rent" is paid. For this reason and many others, the partners should each seek expert advice so that the entire equity-sharing arrangement is structured to fit their individual financial circumstances.

The Amount of Homeowner's Insurance Coverage

Both partners must agree to purchase a homeowner's insurance policy to protect their interests (and the lender's interest) in the property. There are many variations of policies to select from, and the partners should seek the advice of a homeowner's insurance expert.

The Amount of Life Insurance Coverage

The partners should agree to purchase a life insurance policy that covers the outstanding mortgage balance. If one of the partners dies, the mortgage can be paid off with the proceeds of the policy. The contract should also provide for the disposal of the property if one partner dies. For example, the agreement could direct the property to be sold to the public (or to the remaining partner), and the equity distributed between the deceased partner's estate and the surviving partner, pursuant to the disbursement provisions in the agreement.

The Contribution Towards Repairs and Other Cash Expenses

The following are some of the most common contribution variations:

1. Both partners share all cash expenses (repairs, insurance, property taxes).
2. The investor pays all cash expenses, and the insider pays a higher rent.
3. The insider pays all cash expenses and carrying charges, and the investor pays a larger portion of the down payment and closing costs.

The Income Tax Benefits

The IRS has established income tax treatment for real estate investments. To ensure that both partners receive the maximum benefits from their equity sharing arrangement, each party should be represented by experts with experience in equity sharing agreements.

The Depreciation Deduction

The investor, who does not live in the house, is the only partner allowed the depreciation deduction.

The Mortgage Interest Deduction

The agreement for the split of the mortgage interest deduction can be determined in accordance with each partner's contribution during the year. For example, if each party contributes half of the mortgage payment, then each party could claim 50 percent of the mortgage interest deduction.

The Payment of Operating Expenses

Usually the insider is responsible for expenses involving utilities such as heat, electricity, and water since it is the insider who will live in the house and enjoy the benefit of the utilities.

The Split of the Equity When the Arrangement Ends

The value of the property above the mortgage balance is the partners' *equity*. One of the most important terms of an equity sharing agreement is the allocation of that equity when the partnership terminates. This amount is often determined in conjunction with the contributions that each partner makes at the beginning of the partnership. For example, if each partner initially contributes 50 percent towards the down payment and closing costs, then the agreement may call for a 50-50 allocation of the equity that accumulates during the term of the partnership. If the value of the property is $150,000 when it is sold, and the unpaid mortgage balance is $90,000, then the equity in the property is $60,000. In a 50-50 allocation, each partner would be entitled to $30,000. This same concept can be applied to the 90-10 split used in Figure 8-3. In that case, the investor would be entitled to 90 percent of the equity, and the insider would be entitled to 10 percent. Some agreements call for one or both partners to be reimbursed for their original outlay of the down payment and closing costs, after which the remaining equity is divided up according to the distribution percentages that were established.

The Market Value

An accurate market value of the property is essential to the partners when they buy the property, and again when they sell it. The manner in which the appraisals are ordered, the prices that are charged, and the credentials of the appraisal company that will prepare it should be agreed to as part of the equity sharing agreement. One arrangement is that both partners obtain independent appraisals from licensed firms and the property value is established by averaging the two appraisals.

The Buyout Terms

The equity-sharing agreement must provide for the venture to end. As stated previously, equity-sharing arrangements generally last for a term of one to five years. At that point, the equity sharing agreement will be terminated through a prearranged process.

One approach is a buyout arrangement where one of the partners buys out the other partner's interest in the property. The agreement should describe the method for determining the buyout amount, as well as the source of funds that will be used to pay the agreed amount. Will the buying partner have to obtain a new mortgage loan and pay off the original loan so that the selling partner is no longer a party to the original mortgage obligation? Will the buying party be able to keep the existing mortgage loan in place and pay off the other party with cash—and if so, will the lending institution release the selling partner from the mortgage obligation? These details are important because later on, if the buying partner defaults on the mortgage payments, the selling partner, whose name might still be on the mortgage note or bond, could be held responsible for the debt even though he or she is no longer an owner.

If the agreement calls for the premises to be sold to someone other than either partner, these details should be addressed in the agreement. For example, will the house be listed for sale exclusively with one particular real estate broker (an "exclusive" listing), or through an "open" listing, where only the real estate broker who sells the property will earn the commission? Or will the partners try to market and sell the property themselves? Other decisions include the length of time that the listing will be given to a real estate broker and the commission rate to be paid.

Prevention Against Future Borrowing

There should be some agreement between the insider and the investor that the property may not be used as collateral for any future loan

that either partner obtains individually. The agreement should also prohibit a second mortgage on the property, since this could extinguish the
equity that is accumulating.

Protection Against Buyout Option Defaults

There should be some stipulation in the contract about the penalties
that will be incurred if the party who has agreed to buy out the other
party fails to fulfill that obligation in good faith and in a timely fashion.

Payment Defaults

There should be an agreement as to the penalties that will be incurred
should either party default by failing to pay carrying charges, mortgage
payments, other expenses, and so forth.

Dispute Remedies

Both partners should agree to the manner in which they will settle disputes that may arise during the time that they are partners. The choices
can include, but are not limited to, the use of arbitration boards and/or
litigation through the court systems.

The Risks Involved in Equity Sharing

As with any endeavor that involves an investment of money, there are
always risks. Since equity sharing relies on the premise that property values will appreciate, depreciating market prices are one potential
risk. However, because the need for housing continues to rise with
the times, most experts feel that real estate will always be a viable
investment.

If either partner defaults on the agreement, there is the chance that
one partner may have to be responsible for the other partner's portion of the mortgage, in addition to his own. The equity-sharing
agreement may have to be terminated and the property sold, but both
partners would still get the benefit of his or her share of the equity
increase. As the term of ownership lengthens, the risks to the partners
diminishes.

Equity Sharing for Parents and Children

The following example is one in which parents and their child wish to form an equity-sharing arrangement in order to purchase a foreclosure. The parents are looking for a tax shelter, and the child has a good income, but has no cash saved up for the down payment and closing costs.

Let's say the parents and child purchase an REO from a lending institution for $100,000. The property taxes are $2400 per year. They put 10 percent down, and the lending institution has agreed to give them 90 percent financing for 30 years at a 10 percent interest rate. The parents will pay 100 percent of the down payment and closing costs. The child will pay all the monthly carrying charges and will be responsible for completing any repairs. The parents will get 100 percent of the depreciation as a tax benefit and they will split the mortgage interest deduction 50-50 with the child. The parents and child will sell the property in five years and split the equity 50-50 after the sale. Figure 8-3 illustrates the way this will work.

After five years, if the property appreciates at the rate of 5 percent yearly, the new market value is $135,000. The mortgage balance would be approximately $88,000. If the property is sold for $135,000, the equity proceeds of $47,000, would give each of the partners (parents and child) $23,500 in a 50-50 split. In tabular format, this is:

Property value	$135,000 (5% appreciation yearly)
Less: Mortgage balance	($88,000) (approximately)
Equity proceeds	$ 47,000
Split	$ 23,500 each

The parents earned $23,500 from their $19,000 investment, a profit of $4500, which comes to approximately a 4 percent yearly return on their investment. They also benefited from the depreciation and mortgage-interest deductions they claimed on their income tax returns.

The child will now have $23,500 to use as a down payment on another property and will hopefully be able to buy the next home on his or her own.

Equity Sharing for an Investor and a Contractor

Let's look at another type of equity-sharing arrangement, this time between a contractor and an investor. The contractor will be the insider, and will live in the house while making the repairs. The investor will be

Equity-Sharing Arrangement Between Parents and Child

Purchase price:	$100,000
Mortgage amount:	$ 90,000 (*10% interest for 30 years*)
Closing costs:	10% of $90,000 mortgage ($9000)
Yearly property taxes:	$2400
Down payment contribution:	100% (*paid by parents/investors*)
Closing cost contribution:	100% (*paid by parents/investors*)
Carrying charges:	100% (*paid by child/insider*)
Repairs:	100% (*paid by child/insider*)
Tax benefits:	Parents get depreciation
	Mortgage interest is split 50-50
Buyout time:	5 years
Equity split:	50-50

	Parents	Child
Initial Purchase:		
Down payment	$10,000	–
Closing costs	9,000	–
Cash outlay	$19,000	–

	Parents	Child
Monthly carrying:		
Principal/interest	–	$ 789.82
Property taxes	–	$ 200.00
Property insurance	–	$ 50.00
PMI	–	$ 25.00
Total monthly carrying	–	$1,064.82

Figure 8-3. An equity-sharing arrangement between parents and their child.

responsible for the initial cash outlay to cover the down payment and closing costs and the contractor's contribution will be the repairs made to the property.

Unlike the equity sharing arrangement between the parents and child, where the partners must usually wait for their equity to accumulate over time, in the investor and contractor arrangement, the equity accumulation is accelerated because of renovation work that *immediately* improved the value of the property. Therefore, both partners usually agree to sell the property as soon as the repairs are completed.

As illustrated in Figure 8-4, two partners purchase a handyman's special REO from a lending institution for $100,000. The partners put $10,000 down and the lending institution provides financing in the amount of $90,000. The contractor contributes the labor and material, and the investor contributes the down payment and closing costs. In our illustration, $19,000 worth of repairs raises the value of the property from $100,000 to $150,000. The mortgage balance would pretty much remain the same because of the quick sale. Here's how things would work out:

A $30,000 return on a $19,000 investment yields a 57.9 percent return for the investor if the property is sold quickly. In this case the

---

Equity Sharing Between Contractor and Investor

Purchase price	$100,000
Sale price	$150,000
Mortgage balance	$ 90,000
Proceeds	$ 60,000
Split	$ 30,000 each

Figure 8.4 An equity-sharing arrangement between contractor and investor.

partnership agreement should clearly describe a list of the repairs that will be made by the contractor as his or her contribution, as well as the date for completing the work. Another factor that should be confirmed is that the lender will not charge a prepayment penalty if the partners pay off the loan within the first couple of months.

Finding a Partner for Equity Sharing

An Inside Occupant Who is Looking for an Investor as a Partner Should Do the Following:

- Make an appointment with your attorney, your accountant, and/or your financial advisor to work out a plan that enhances your monetary needs.

- To attract investors, put an ad in your local newspaper, such as: *"Only $19,000 buys 90 percent ownership of income-producing property. Investor's dream: 90 percent profit when sold—0 percent headaches of being a landlord. Positive cash flow monthly. Call Mr. Averageson at (212) 555-1000."*

- Look in the classified section of your local newspaper under such headings as "Money to Lend." Investors with money for this sort of venture may advertise there.

- When you find an investor to work with, set up an appointment to discuss your intentions and to outline a plan of action regarding the cost of the property you wish to purchase and the contribution you will be making. You will also need to structure the tax deductions, the monthly payment setup, and the buyout terms.

- Both partners should meet together with their attorneys, accountants, and/or tax advisors to ensure that everyone's intentions are clear and everyone's interests are protected.

- Inspect and select the property that is right for you and enter into a formal contract.

- File your mortgage application, close, and move in.

The Outside Investor Looking for an Insider as a Partner Should Do the Following:

- Consult your tax advisor or attorney to review the tax consequences for your role in equity sharing, as well as your capital requirements and availability of funds.

- *Put an ad in your local newspaper to attract an insider, as follows: "No cash down buys 10 percent ownership of 8-room high-ranch in Any County, USA. Payments each month equal rent of $_____. No need to qualify for a mortgage. Call Ms. Welloff at (201) 555-2000."*

- When you find an insider who will work with you, it may be advisable to request a credit report to ensure that he or she would make a credit-worthy partner.

- When you find an insider to work with, outline a plan of action regarding the cost of the property you wish to purchase and the contribution you will be making. You will also need to agree to the tax deductions, the monthly payment setup, and the buyout terms.

- Both partners should meet together with their attorneys, accountants, and/or tax advisors to ensure that everyone's intentions are clear and everyone's interests are protected.

- Inspect and select the property that is right for you and enter into a formal contract.

- File the mortgage application and close on the property.

Equity Sharing Helps People Achieve Their Goals

Equity sharing satisfies the needs of an investor who wants to buy a fore-closure to use as a rental property, and who wants the added security of a good tenant. It also satisfies the needs of a prospective home buyer who would like to purchase a foreclosure to live in, but who does not currently have the finances to do so independently.

9

Choosing the Right Property: What You Don't Know *Can* Hurt You

Most foreclosures are sold in "as-is" condition. This wording places buyers "on notice" that they are waiving the "built-in" warrantees (i.e., that the fixtures, appliances, heating, lighting, and electrical systems, etc., are in good working order) that they might normally take for granted in traditional purchases. While an "as-is" condition disclaimer can leave foreclosure buyers vulnerable to "problem" properties, forewarned is also forearmed, and purchasers who are aware of their responsibility to protect their interests will (hopefully) be more diligent in their research and in calculating their bid limits.

Ascertaining the condition of the property is just one of the preliminary preparations for selecting foreclosed properties. Chapter 9 introduces readers to the homework, legwork, and research skills that play an essential role in determining which properties are worth pursuing.

Finding the Right Price

Before you spend valuable time looking for foreclosures that you *think* you can afford, your first preliminary preparation is to *know* how much money you have available to go shopping with. Why waste time and energy on properties that are too expensive, or pass up a great opportunity that you didn't realize was in your price range?

The two procedures that lenders perform in order to "take your financial temperature" are *prequalifications* and *preapprovals*. The distinctions between the two are especially crucial when time is a critical factor and you need the money to purchase the property quickly.

Prequalified versus Preapproved

Although many purchasers and even people in the financial industry use the terms interchangeably, there is a big difference between a prequalification and a preapproval.

A *prequalification* is not much more than an "over-the-phone" estimate from a lender of the interest rate, points, etc., that you will pay, as well as the maximum loan you can apply for, based on your income and credit. *If* everything you say is true, and *if* there are no credit problems, the lender will loan you the money at the rate and terms they quoted you. Prequalifications are conditional upon everything—your income, credit history, the amount in your bank accounts, etc. Nothing has been verified, and you would first begin the steps for applying for a mortgage after you receive the purchase contract from the seller.

A *preapproval*, on the other hand, gives the borrower and the lender a much more accurate picture of the applicant's financial status, which accelerates the time frame for getting the loan commitment. The same information is required as for a prequalification, including income verification, credit history, bank accounts, etc., but unlike a prequalification procedure, the lender processes the application forms and issues a commitment *before* the applicant has even bid or made an offer for a foreclosure. Truly authentic preapprovals are those that are signed by an underwriter, who issues a certificate guaranteeing the amount and terms of the loan. The only conditions that still must be met for the lender to close are the appraisal and the title report, which *can* be completed within a couple of weeks. The applicant can now focus on foreclosures to purchase within his or her price range, and once the applicant goes to contract, the only things left to do are ordering the appraisal and the title search. Why is this important? There are two reasons. First, when you purchase a foreclosure at an auction, you may be able to get financing from a bank within the 30-day period between the signing of the contract and the closing because you were already preapproved by the lender before you bid on the property, and it is realistic to assume that the appraisal and the title report can be completed by the lender in time for the closing. Secondly, bank and government agencies, as well as delinquent owners, take a prospective purchaser's offer very seriously when the purchaser is already preapproved and ready to close quickly.

The downside of a preapproval is that, unless you don't need to inspect the house because you plan to rip it down and rebuild it, there may be delays in getting the financing approved if, for example, utilities are not operating, the house is in need of a lot of repair work, or there are unfriendly occupants living in the house who won't allow a bank representative inside to inspect (or appraise) it. In any of those cases, the lender is unlikely to approve the loan until the premises can be inspected by the bank's appraiser. In some cases, the lender won't approve the loan when the bank appraiser's report shows that there are extensive repairs needed. In other words, you may be limited to selecting foreclosed properties that are accessible and in good condition.

Questions to Ask a Lender When Shopping for a Preapproval

- Once you are preapproved, what are the additional conditions that must be met in order for you to get the financing? (Authentic preapprovals are already signed by an underwriter, and only require a title report and an appraisal.)

- Is there a fee for the preapproval, and how much is it? (Usually no fee)
- How long does the preapproval process take to complete? (Usually five to eight business days)
- How long is the preapproval good for? (Usually 60 to 90 days from commitment)
- If the preapproval expires, is there a fee to renew it? (Maybe)

Finding the Right Property

You will need to inspect the properties that you are interested in, ask questions of certain people and agencies, and research the market conditions in your preferred locale before you attend any auctions or present any written offers. These preliminary preparations are the best way for buyers to uncover costly problems and to ensure accuracy in calculating the amount to pay for the property. The results of your inspections and research, along with the answers to your questions, will help you accurately distinguish a "dream" from a "disaster."

Getting Access

Your first step is to contact the referee, the foreclosing lender's attorney, the real estate broker, or other designated authority for access to the premises. You may be told, "You can inspect the property on Saturday at 3:00," or you may be told, "If you can get past the pit bull and the guy with the shotgun, be my guest!" In any event, be prepared to make your inspection.

The Preliminary Inspection

Foreclosure properties are found in four basic conditions:

- *Vacant and accessible*. No one lives there, and you can go inside and inspect the premises.
- *Occupied and accessible*. Someone lives there and allows you inside to inspect the premises.
- *Vacant and inaccessible*. No one lives there and there is no access to inspect the premises.

- *Occupied and inaccessible*. An unfriendly, angry occupant lives there and answers the door to greet you with his rabid pit bull and his loaded shotgun.

Keep in mind that the purpose of your inspection is to identify potential problems and additional expenses, and to gather information to help you calculate your bid limits. You will need to bring a pen or a pencil. (Forget about ballpoint pens in cold weather—the pens freeze and will not write properly.) Bring a camera for taking pictures of the properties, and a notepad for writing your observations about each property as you are performing your inspection. If you will be inspecting five or six properties, the most important thing you can do is to take *specific* notes about each one on a separate inspection form. You will *never* be able to remember all the details of each property unless you write down as much information as possible. To help you keep track of which notes go with which property, attach the pictures you take to each inspection sheet you prepare. The important things to look at (in addition to the cosmetic appearance and the plumbing, heating, and electrical systems) are: the structure itself; structural and cosmetic improvements such as a shed, an in-ground pool, the detached new garage, the second-story extension that looks like it was recently added; and anything else that may affect either the marketability or value of the property. For efficiency and expediency, an instamatic camera or a digital camera that can provide you with an immediate image is recommended. (Imagine shooting an entire roll of film and finding out later that it didn't develop properly. Now, imagine how annoyed you will be when you have to go back and shoot everything all over again!) A flashlight or battery-operated lantern is also recommended because, in many cases, the electrical system will eventually be disconnected after the last occupants vacate the property. Even if the electricity is working, you may still wish to illuminate areas within the property that are dimly lit in order to get a better view of the condition of the property.

   Keep the pictures and the notes you have taken accessible for later on, when you contact the various parties that are mentioned throughout this chapter. But first, I just want to give you a few words of advice before you perform your inspections.

Life-Saving Safety Tips for Inspections

No Smoking. When you are inspecting vacant properties as part of your preliminary preparations for bidding, *never enter a vacant house carrying a lit cigarette.* There may be a gas leak that no one is aware of (since no one lives there), and a lit cigarette could cause an explosion of life-threatening proportions.

Don't Go Alone. Vacant houses can attract vandals or vagrants. Do not inspect the properties that you are interested in alone. Besides, two people are more likely to notice and remember important details about the properties you inspect. For the most efficient planning, bring your contractor and/or engineer with you, and ask them to give you written estimates for the repairs.

Protect Yourself. Another tip is illustrated by my own personal experience. After we inspected a vacant foreclosure, my assistant noticed something on my clothes, and pointed it out to me. I looked down and saw hundreds of small dots all over my white skirt. (It's a good thing it was summertime and that I was wearing a light-colored skirt!) Then, I realized that the itching I was feeling wasn't imaginary, and that those little dots were moving! Fleas! Hundreds of fleas all over me! It seemed at the time that the fleas were waiting for someone's legs to present themselves for dinner. If my assistant hadn't noticed something on my skirt, I would have infested my car, my dog, and consequently, my home. Finding yourself in such a situation is a nightmare, and can be especially dangerous for people who are allergic to fleabites. The point is, remember to bring insect repellent and to wear protective clothing (or at least put rubber bands around the bottom of your pants legs) in order to keep these, or other annoying creatures from crawling under your garments.

Once Is Not Enough

I suggest that you visit the properties you are interested in at different times of the day and in different weather conditions. Does the property flood during a heavy rain? Is the area surrounding the property a local hangout for noisy teenagers? Is the property near a body of water that might cause flooding or other problems at high tide? One bank representative told me about an REO situated on a canal that had recently been repossessed by the bank he worked for. Potential purchasers came to inspect the property in the morning, liked it, and put down a deposit. When they came back later in the afternoon, the high tide from the morning was gone, and they found fish all over the front lawn and rescinded their offer! Don't stop now; there are other things to look for. Is there a railroad line nearby, and when the train comes through does it shake the pictures off the wall and transform the bath water into a whirlpool? Your inspections may result in some very disturbing findings, or in great news that the property is worth pursuing.

Asking the Right Questions

Your physical inspection of the properties will provide you with a foundation to begin your calculations. The questions that follow can help you identify costly expenses and prevent costly mistakes.

Questions to Ask the Foreclosing Lender's Attorney, Referee, Real Estate Broker, Property Manager, or Other Designated Official

- *How do you obtain access to the properties in order to conduct an inspection?*
  For access to properties that will be sold at upcoming auctions, contact the foreclosing lender or referee. (The names are usually included in legal notices, commercial foreclosure lists, etc.) *For access to bank-owned and government-owned foreclosures,* contact the real estate broker or designated property manager. (Names and contact information are usually included in REO and government agency lists and advertisements.) *For access to preforeclosures,* contact the delinquent homeowners.

- *Are the utilities operating, and has the plumbing system been winterized (in cold climates)?*
  In order to obtain financing, most lenders will send a bank representative (i.e., the bank appraiser) to inspect the plumbing, heating, and electric systems and confirm that they are in good working order. If, for example, the plumbing system has been winterized to prevent frozen pipes (in colder climates), the system cannot be tested properly, and the loan may be delayed or denied. After the contract is signed, the seller may have to dewinterize the plumbing system so that the lender can complete its inspection. Similarly, the sellers may have to contact utility companies (i.e., electric and gas providers) and heating suppliers to have them restore services so that the other related systems can also be inspected. Even if you are not expecting to obtain financing from a lender (i.e., you are paying cash at the auction), you still want to have the systems turned on to calculate the costs of repairs that may be needed.

- *Has the house been boarded up?*
  If the premises are boarded up (entry doors and window glass were removed and replaced with plywood to protect against vandalism), you will have to bring sufficient supplemental lighting devices (i.e., lanterns) in order to perform your inspection. (There is nothing darker—or for that matter, colder—than a boarded-up house.) Another

issue to address is the whereabouts of the entry doors and window glass that were removed. If the property is sold "as is," the new owner would most likely have to pay for replacing the doors and windows. Were they stored in the garage in the backyard? Or if the property is an REO, maybe the bank has a storage facility where the windows and doors were taken. In any event, unless the seller is willing to guarantee in writing that the doors and windows will be provided, the costs for replacing them should be included as part of your bid calculations.

- **What form of down payment is required?**

  Contact the referee or the foreclosing lender's attorney and ask what form the down payment must be in. Whether you are purchasing a bank foreclosure at an auction, an REO from a lender or a government agency, or a preforeclosure from a delinquent homeowner, the down payment generally must be in the form of a certified check, attorney's check, cashier's check, or a money order. Cash may also be acceptable in some cases.

- **When is the closing date?**

  Usually, in foreclosure auctions the closing is completed within 30 days of the day that the property was awarded to the high bidder, and the contract signed. On the other hand, if you are purchasing a bank or government REO and the bank that owns the property agrees to provide financing, then the closing date will be set once the financing is approved by the bank.

- **Will I lose my down payment if I fail to close?**

  If you purchased the property at an auction and are unable to close in the 30-day period stipulated in the referee's contract, in most cases, the down payment will not be refundable if failure to close is the fault of the high bidder. But if the foreclosing lender is unable to close for some reason, there is a possibility that the down payment might be refunded. Reasons may include, but are not limited to, improper service of legal documents on the delinquent borrower at the time the foreclosure action first began, additional liens and judgments that have been discovered that were accidentally omitted from the upset price (which could cause the upset price to be substantially higher), or the foreclosing lender's inability to provide the necessary legal documents. If the down payment is refundable, you will also want to know how long it will take for you to recover your money.

- **Is there a Torrens title or a regular deed, and is it available or on file with the foreclosing lender?**

  As discussed previously in Chapter 2, information concerning the deed would be included in the title report that was ordered by the foreclosing lender's attorney when the foreclosure action was first initiated.

■ *Is the contract assignable?*

Contracts are normally automatically assignable, unless there is wording in the contract that forbids assignment. Usually, contracts for the sale of real estate where the financing is not contingent upon the buyer's income and credit rating can be assigned to another buyer, as long as that buyer has enough cash to close. For example, you may find assignable contracts at mortgage foreclosure auctions—where the contract terms do not allow down payment refunds if a buyer is unable to obtain financing. Even when the contract is assignable, however, the original party is still obligated to complete the transaction if the party to whom the contract was assigned fails to do so. By contrast, when a buyer is purchasing an REO from a lender's inventory, and the lender is providing the financing, the loan's approval is contingent upon the buyer's income and credit rating, and therefore, the buyer's contract with the lender for the REO is unlikely to be assignable.

■ *Who is responsible for the protection of the premises between the contract and closing dates?*

In most cases, the foreclosing lender cannot protect the premises or give any guarantees about its condition if there are people occupying the property. If the property is vacant, however, the foreclosing lender's insurance policy should cover any additional damages that occur between contract and closing.

■ *Who is responsible for major structural repairs?*

If you are purchasing the property at an auction, in most cases, you are responsible. Remember, you are purchasing the property in "as-is" condition. If you are purchasing an REO or a property that is owned by a government agency, however, you may be able to get financial assistance for repairs. I was once involved with an REO purchase in which the bank that owned it issued a $500 credit at the closing for the purchaser to repair a collapsed cesspool.

■ *What is the status of the current occupants?*

If you are the highest bidder at an auction and there are people currently living in the property, you will probably be responsible for the eviction procedures once you are the new owner. Sometimes the occupants have already advised the foreclosing lender that they will be moving out voluntarily. This may help you to be more accurate when you prepare your bid amount because you will know whether or not you can eliminate eviction costs from your bid calculations. If you are purchasing an REO from a lender's inventory, the property may have already been vacated. Some lenders with REOs in their inventories evict the occupants as a prerequisite to putting the property on the market.

- *Is prepossession allowed prior to closing if you are in contract?*

Ask if prepossession is allowed during the period of time between the contract and the closing. If the premises are vacant, you may want to begin making repairs in order to rent it to tenants or to resell it more quickly than if you waited until after the closing. On the other hand, if you plan to live in the property and it is in good enough condition, you may want to move in yourself. Prepossession may also be granted by lending institutions for their REOs. The lending institutions may find this to be beneficial, especially when the property is vacant, as a means of avoiding vandalism.

There are some issues that may arise in connection with prepossession. In some cases, the seller may want you to pay "rent" for the period of time you take possession up until the closing date. In that case, you would have to weigh the benefits you gain from prepossession against the rental expense.

Some attorneys advise sellers and purchasers against prepossession because of the risk that something could go wrong during the financing and title processes that could interfere with the closing and invalidate the sale (i.e., financing is denied, unexpected title problems, etc.). In that situation, unless there was a specific provision in the contract terms to repay the prepossessor for labor and materials, it may be difficult, if not impossible, for the prepossessor to recover any repair costs that he or she had expended. You might consider incorporating a repayment agreement into the contract whereby the seller agrees to pay a preagreed price for completing specific work, in the event that the closing is called off.

After both parties sign the contract, the purchaser, by virtue of paying the down payment, has an insurable interest in the property. Whereas normally, you would expect to obtain property insurance that is effective on the day of the closing, if you are granted permission to take possession prior to closing, a crucial part of your rental agreement with the seller would be to ensure that the premises are covered against losses. Many times, you will be required to provide your own property insurance coverage that is effective on the date you are taking prepossession.

- *Does the foreclosed owner's "right-of-redemption" survive the auction?*

In a mortgage foreclosure action in some states, the previous owner's right of redemption is extinguished once the bidding begins. In other states, the owner's right of redemption may survive the auction, which means that even after the property is awarded to the highest bidder, for a limited period of time, the previous owner can still pay the upset price and redeem ownership of the premises.

■ *Are there any additional liens or judgments attached to the premises?*

Ask if there are any additional liens or judgments attached to the premises for which you would be held responsible, in addition to the purchase price. This question is especially important in auction situations where a diligent search of the public records in the county clerk's office is an essential preliminary preparation. By contrast, in most REO cases, the bank clears the title once the property comes back into its inventory, by paying off the outstanding liens and judgments.

Questions To Ask the Town/City Hall (Where the Foreclosure Is Located)

■ *Is there an existing certificate of occupancy (or its equivalent) on file?*

Contact (or visit) the town hall (or appropriate government agency) in the town where the property is located, and ask for a copy of the latest certificate of occupancy (CO) that is on file there. A certificate of occupancy (or its equivalent) is issued by a town's (or another government agency's) building department and certifies that the construction of the dwelling was done in accordance with local building codes. An example of a certificate of occupancy is included as Figure 9-1.

■ *Is there an updated survey on file?*

Contact or visit the building department (or appropriate government agency) in the town where the property is located and ask for a copy of the latest survey that is on file there. A survey is an illustration of the property description. Figure 9-2 is an example of a survey for a property that was improved with a two-story dwelling.

Now compare your pictures from your preliminary property inspection to the certificate of occupancy and the survey. Make sure that all additional structures are accounted for. Sure, you may have always dreamed of that in-ground pool, and the deck that was added *looks* pretty sturdy, but if these improvements violate the building codes in your area, or if they have not yet been inspected and approved by the property authorities, you could be in for some costly problems. In most states, a certificate of occupancy or its equivalent, along with an updated survey, are required in order for you to get a mortgage loan. Even if you are buying the property at the auction with cash, and you don't need a mortgage loan, whoever you sell the property to in later years will probably need a mortgage loan and will be unable to get one unless these documents can be produced.

BUILDING DEPARTMENT
TOWN OF SMITHTOWN
SUFFOLK COUNTY, N.Y.

CERTIFICATE OF OCCUPANCY COMPLIANCE

This certifies that the .... Building ....

located at S/S New Highway, Valmont Village, Sec. # 5 ....

....

....

Described .... Map No. .... Block .... Lot No. ....

Conforms substantially with the terms and requirements of the New York State Building Code and

Town of Smithtown Zoning Ordinance, as amended to date, and may be permitted to be used and

occupied as a . One Family Dwelling 43.6 x 24.8 with 2 car att/garage ....

Subject to the following conditions: ....

....

....

Owner Melody Construction, Inc. Commack, NY ....

Signed ..... Harvey R. Manuel

BUILDING OFFICIAL

The building or any part there of shall not be used for any purposes other than for which it is certified. Cerficate will be null and void if this building is altered in any manner or additions are made thereto without authorization from the Building Department.

COPY

Figure 9-1. A certificate of occupancy.

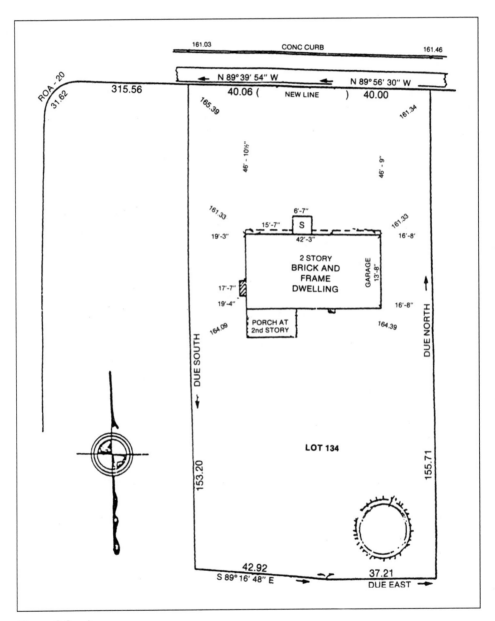

Figure 9-2. A survey.

Many foreclosure purchasers will still bid on property with incomplete or missing documents. When they are calculating their bids, they simply take into consideration the costs that they will incur to obtain these documents. For example, let's say you are interested in property with an in-ground pool, but the previous owners never applied for the proper permits, and there is no certificate of occupancy to confirm that the pool was built in accordance with local building codes. While this situation seems like it could be highly problematic, your preliminary preparations for determining whether or not to pursue this property can be broken down into four steps. First, arrange to meet the local building inspector at the property, so that you can ascertain specifically what repairs will be required (i.e., fences, electrical work, and so forth) in order to satisfy the building codes so that the certificate of occupancy can be issued for the pool. Second, get a written estimate from a licensed contractor for any repairs that you would have to do in conjunction with the building inspector's report. Third, contact the local property tax collector to find out if there will be a significant increase in the property taxes once the improvements are completed and the certificate of occupancy is issued. Fourth, get a price from a surveyor for the cost of preparing an updated survey that will include the in-ground pool.

Many people feel that purchasing a property for a fraction of its actual value is well worthwhile, even if some legwork is required to research and obtain the missing documents.

- *Does the local government require a rental permit for you to rent out the property that you are interested in, and is there a rental permit currently in effect?*

Some government zoning agencies require the owner of a rental property (yes, even a single-family rental property) to obtain a rental permit before tenants can move in. The procedure may simply involve filing an application with the local building department and paying an annual (or biannual) rental permit fee. A physical inspection by a building inspector may also be required to ensure that the premises that are being rented out are fit for human habitation. Because procedures vary from location to location, investors should contact the local zoning authorities for information about the procedure that is followed in the area where they wish to purchase foreclosures.

- *Are there any private deed or public zoning restrictions that could affect the current or future use of the premises by new owners or their tenants?*

Here are some examples of private deed restrictions or public zoning restrictions that could cause problems for future owners.

  - A town with a rental permit requirement could pose a problem if the town has called a moratorium (a temporary halt) on issuing rental permits and you want to purchase an investment property in that town to rent out to tenants.

- There could be a restriction that prohibits parking of commercial vehicles on the premises. This could cause problems for people with commercial vehicles who would have to find an alternate place to park their commercial vehicles when they are not working, and who will need noncommercial vehicles to get back and forth from their homes to the place they park their vehicles each day.

- There could be a restriction that controls the color and type of paint that must be used to repaint the exterior of the house, and prospective buyers may not happy with any of the colors that they can choose from.

- In older homes, there could be a restriction on changing the exterior of the house if the premises are designated as a landmark of historical significance.

- There could be a private easement that allows a neighboring owner to use the property you are interested in purchasing for access to and from his landlocked residence.

Questions To Ask the Utility Companies (that Service the Premises)

- *Are there currently any outstanding utility debts?*

    Contact the utility companies that service the premises (for example, water, gas, and electricity) and ask if there are currently any outstanding utility debts. If there are, ask who is responsible for payment. Would you, as the new owner, have to pay off the arrears in order to reinstate service. The amount due may be substantial or it may be negligible, but in either case, knowing this amount will help you figure out your bid amount since you will be incorporating all of your expenses into your final calculations.

- *Are there any incomplete community services?*

    If you are purchasing property with an incomplete sewer hookup you may run into a huge expense if the property is located a lengthy distance from the main sewer line connection. The same situation may occur in areas where well water is being replaced with city or community water services. If you are able to purchase the property for a low enough price, just incorporate the amount you will need for completing the hookup into your bid amount.

Organizing Yourself

Figure 9-3 is a checklist that you can use as a framework for the questions you will need to ask about the properties you are interested in. This checklist is not intended to be all-inclusive. You may need to obtain additional information from other sources.

Inspecting the File of the Foreclosure Action

Contact the designated authority handling the foreclosure action and ask about access to the files that are part of the action. In most cases, these files are public records open for examination by the public at large. Most of the time, these files are stored somewhere in the county center in the county where the property is located. Files are usually requisitioned by index number. The index number usually appears in the legal notices that are publicized as part of the foreclosure procedure.

Hiring a Title Expert

Many people without experience in real estate title work feel unsure of their ability to ascertain that the property they are interested in is really a good choice. If you feel intimidated about asking questions, or if you feel unsure of yourself and lack confidence in your ability to do the preliminary investigation work that's required, I strongly recommend that you hire a title (or foreclosure) expert to search the records you will need and to give you many of the answers that will help you determine if the property is right for you. Title experts are equipped to handle most of the work discussed here, like last-owner searches, and they can direct you to other experts for answers to your questions.

Asking for the "Terms of Sale" Before Bidding on Foreclosures at Auctions

In addition to asking your questions, if you plan on buying your foreclosure at an auction, I advise you to ask the foreclosing lender's attorney or the referee for an advance copy of the contract that will be provided to the successful high bidder. In this way, your attorney can help you

Prebid Questions

Foreclosing Lender's Attorney/Referee/Real Estate Broker/ Designated Authority:

- Will there be access to the premises for inspection before bidding?
- What is the status of the utilities (heating, electric, etc.)?
- Has the plumbing system been winterized?
- Has the house been boarded up?
- If boarded up, where are the doors and windows that were removed?
- What form must the down payment be in?
- When is the required closing date?
- Will I lose my down payment if I fail to close?
- Is there a Torrens title or a regular deed available?
- Is the contract assignable?
- Who is responsible for protection of the premises?
- Are there any credits given (off the sales price) for major structural repairs?
- Is prepossession allowed prior to closing?
- Are there any additional liens or judgments attached to the premises?

Building Department (Where the Premises Are Located):

- Is there a certificate of occupancy (or its equivalent) available?
- Is there an updated survey available?
- Is there a rental permit requirement for the township?
- Is there a current rental permit on file?
- Are there private or zoning restrictions that affect future owners?

Utility companies (That Service the Premises):

- Are there currently any outstanding utility debts?
- Who is responsible for paying these outstanding utility debts?
- Are there any incomplete services (such as sewer or city water hookups)?

PLEASE NOTE: NOT ALL-INCLUSIVE—ADDITIONAL INFORMATION MAY BE REQUIRED

Figure 9-3.   A sample checklist of prebid questions.

preview the contract terms and identify any stipulations that may cause problems, such as penalties for not closing and the like.

Uncovering Hidden Costs

When you are choosing the property that is right for you, you will need to know some of the hidden costs they may not have warned you about on those late-night television infomercials. As is true for most real estate transactions, your actual expenses are more than just the purchase price of the property. Here are some additional costs that you should expect when you are considering a foreclosure purchase.

A Homeowner's Insurance Policy

One of the additional expenses in the purchase of a property is the expense of insuring it. If you intend to live there, you will need a ***homeowner's insurance policy*** to protect your interests in the property as an owner-occupant.

If you intend to rent the property to tenants, you will need a ***landlord's policy*** that provides a different type of coverage. Years ago, an investor told me about a rental property that he had just renovated at a cost of thousands of dollars. One week before the tenants were scheduled to move in, someone broke into the basement and completely destroyed the heating unit with a sledgehammer. The investor was not covered by his insurance. He *would have* been covered if the person who had broken into the house had *removed* the heating unit, because the investor had coverage for theft, but unfortunately, he didn't have vandalism insurance, and was unable to recover the losses he sustained. Landlords have special insurance needs that owner-occupants do not have. Chose an insurance provider who is experienced with landlord policies, and who can explain the coverage that best protects your investment.

For investors who wish to rent out their property to others, *a rent-loss policy* is also recommended. In the event that a disaster, such as a fire, forces your tenant to vacate the premises, this rent-loss policy (like business interruption insurance) should insure you for lost rental income while your property is being repaired. Will this type of insurance cover you for a deadbeat tenant who doesn't feel like paying the rent? Unfortunately, this policy is not for that type of "rent loss." However, let's say you *do* have a fire in a house you rent out to others. You call the bank that holds your mortgage and you say, "Hello, XYZ Bank? We just had a fire in the house and the tenants had to move out. We won't be receiving any rental income for a while, so we won't be able to make the mortgage payments for a few months or so, okay?" What will XYZ Bank say? "See you at the foreclosure." This rent-loss insurance policy will cover the lost rental payments so that you can continue to pay your mortgage.

Another insurance expense is *title insurance*. In almost all real estate purchases, you will need to obtain title insurance to help protect you against title claims. Your attorney can help you choose the proper coverage.

If you are planning to rent the house out to others, it is best to qualify the prospective tenants and their ability to pay the rent each month. But what if the tenants have an accident and are unable to work? How are they going to pay the rent? Now you are stuck in the uncomfortable position of dealing with an injured tenant who can't pay you, as well as the possibility of a costly and lengthy eviction procedure. I suggest a *tenant's disability policy,* which provides coverage for tenants in the event that they become disabled and are unable to pay the rent. The cost of this type of policy will vary according to the amount of coverage and the tenant's age, sex, and occupation; however, the cost can be as low as a few dollars a month. You can have your tenant buy the policy and name you (the landlord) as the beneficiary, or you can buy the policy for the tenant and be named as both the owner of the policy and the beneficiary. This may qualify for a tax deduction as a landlord's expense.

If you intend to live in the premises, then a *mortgage disability policy* is suggested. What if you have an accident and are unable to work? Who will pay your mortgage? Will you be foreclosed on? A mortgage disability policy is another insurance policy to consider when buying a foreclosure or any other type of real estate.

Missing Property Documents

You may incur additional expenses if you must procure missing documents in order to purchase your foreclosure.

If you need a *survey,* the building department in the town (or city) hall where the premises are located may already have this document on file. There is usually a minimal fee to obtain a copy. If the existing survey is more than 10 years old, or if there were improvements to the premises that affect the structure, and do not appear on the original survey (such as a deck, an in-ground pool, or a new detached garage), you will need to have a new survey prepared. This may be an expensive undertaking. Remember, there is no obligation for the foreclosing lender to provide you with a new survey if you are purchasing the property "as is" at an auction.

The *Certificate of Occupancy* (or related proof of structural approval) should also be on file with the town (or city) building department in the town (or city) where the premises are located. If a new CO is required, the normal procedure for obtaining one includes a visit from the appropriate inspector. The inspector will examine the premises to make sure that any additions or improvements were constructed in accordance with the local building codes. There may be additional violations that that will require costly repairs. These violations may not even have been applicable at the time that the structure was originally completed, but new, updated services may be required under current building codes.

If you plan to rent the property out to others, you may need a *rental permit*. The permit procedure is often implemented by local government agencies, such as the town building department, to protect potential tenants from substandard living conditions. An inspection by the local building department and a fee for the permit may also be required.

Outstanding Utility Expenses

Additional utility expenses include water, electric, and gas charges that may have accrued under the previous owner, or deposits that the utility company requires from new owners who wish to reinstate service. Cesspool certifications, well tests, and sewer hookups also fall into this category.

Repair Costs

The repair costs include both structural and cosmetic repairs, per the reports given to you by your licensed contractor or engineer. Figure 9-4 is an example of an engineer's report. Going forward, Chapter 13 shows you how to hire and work with your contractor.

Eviction Costs

The burden of evicting the existing occupants from the premises may be on you, as the new owner, unless otherwise agreed. This will include court costs and legal fees, naturally, and if you are buying the foreclosure as an investor, don't forget to include the rent loss sustained during the eviction period.

Unpaid Property Taxes

The upset price of a property purchased at an auction usually includes the amount of the unpaid property taxes. However, you may be responsible for the amount of property taxes that have accrued from the date of the auction until the day you close (approximately 30 days). This is because the property tax arrears can only be figured accurately for the period that the delinquency began, until the date of the auction. Thus, if we have an

SAMPLE OF AN ENGINEER'S REPORT

I. OUTSIDE

1. GRADING: Good ☐ Fair☐ Poor ☐ Low Spots: Yes___; 2. NO. ELECT. WIRES___Over☐ Under ☐ Capacity___Amps
2. TERMITES: None Apparent ☐ Evidences of ☐ : _____
3. EXTERIOR WALLS: Material_____
   Repairs Needed: Yes ☐ _____
4. ROOFING: Material: _____ Age: _____Years
   Repairs Needed: Yes ☐ _____
5. GUTTERS & LEADERS: Material_____ Drains/Drywells; Yes☐ No ☐ ; Repair/Replacement:_____

II. SUPPORT STRUCTURE: MECHANICAL/ELECTRICAL

1. BSMT: Full ☐ Partial☐ CRAWL: ☐ SLAB: ☐ Full ☐ Partial ☐_____
2. WATER PENETRATION: Seepage ☐ Dampness ☐_____
3. FLOOR: Concrete ☐ Wood ☐ Dirt ☐ ; Cracks: Some ☐ Many ☐   Texture: Smooth ☐ Rough ☐   Floor Drains: Yes☐
4. TERMITES: None Apparent ☐ Evidences of ☐ : _____
5. FOUNDATION WALLS: Material_____Condition_____Cracks: Yes ☐ No ☐ Not Visible ☐
6. COLUMNS: Material_____(Not) (Part) Visible ☐ Condition_____
7. GIRDERS: Material_____(Not) (Part) Visible ☐ Condition_____
8. FLOOR JOISTS: Size/Spacing/Span_____(Not) (Few) Visible ☐ Condition _____
9. HEATING SYSTEM: Hot Water ☐ Hot Air ☐ Steam ☐ ; Fuel: Gas☐ Oil☐ Elect. ☐ ; No. of Zones____Vented: Yes☐ No☐

III. ATTIC AREA

1. ROOF RAFTERS: Size & Spacing_____ Standard ☐ Below Standard ☐   Evidences of Rot: Yes☐ No ☐
2. INSULATION: Floor ☐ Walls ☐ Roof ☐ None ☐   Vapor Barrier: Yes ☐ No ☐ · Type and Thickness _____
3. FLOOR JOISTS: Size & Spacing:_____Can Accommodate Normal Storage: Yes ☐ No ☐   Flooring: Yes ☐ No ☐ Partial ☐
4. VENTILATION: Adequate ☐ More Needed ☐ None ☐   5. LEAKS, Condensation: Yes ☐ No ☐_____

ROOM: _____

1. CEILING: Plaster ☐ Drywall ☐ Paneling ☐ Other ☐ _____ Cracks: Yes ☐ Leaks: Yes ☐ _____
2. WALLS: Plaster ☐ Drywall ☐ Paneling ☐ Tiles ☐ Other ☐ _____ Cracks: Yes ☐ Leaks: Yes ☐ _____
3. WINDOWS: No. ____Type: Double Hung ☐ Casement ☐ Slider ☐ Jalousie ☐; Material: Wood ☐ Metal ☐ Vinyl ☐
                Wth'r. Stpd.:Yes ☐ No ☐ Cords Broken: Yes ☐ Insulated Glass ☐ Single Glass ☐ Storm: Yes ☐ No ☐
4. ELECTRIC OUTLETS: No._____ Wall Switches: Yes ☐ No ☐ Old ☐
5. FLOOR: Wood _____Tile ☐ Concrete ☐ Covered ☐ Condition: Acceptable ☐ Needs Repair ☐ Slopes ☐ Squeaks ☐
6. TRIM: Wood ☐ Tile☐ Steel ☐   Condition: Acceptable ☐ Needs Repair/Upgrading_____
7. HARDWARE: (Hinges, Locks, Knobs, etc.):   Condition: Good ☐ Functional ☐ Old ☐ Need Repair ☐
8. HEATING: Radiators____Convectors ____Heat Grills ____ A/C Grill ____ Baseboard ☐ Radiant Htg. ☐ Pipe Riser ☐
9. DOORS: Exterior:_____ Good ☐ Acceptable ☐ Poor ☐ Repair/Replace _____
                Interior: _____ Good ☐ Acceptable ☐ Poor ☐ Repair/Replace _____
10. PLUMBING FIXTURES: Good ☐ Operating ☐ Replace_____ Faucet Leaks: Yes ☐ _____Sink Drains_____
                Pressure: Normal ☐ Below Normal☐ Tile Repairs Needed at Tub/Shower: Yes _____
11. APPLIANCES: STOVE: Gas ☐___ Elect.☐___REFRIGERATOR: None ☐ Operating ☐ Old ☐_____
                DISHWASHER: Functional ☐ Old ☐   Other_____

For more information, contact Taucher-Chronacker Professional Engineers (516) 766-1019

Figure 9-4.   A sample engineer's report.

expected closing period of 30 days between the auction date and the closing date, and property taxes are $2400 per year, the costs can be calculated at $200. On the other hand, when purchasing an REO, your property tax responsibility begins on the day you close on the property.

Establishing Property Values

When you're choosing the property that is right for you, one of your primary concerns will be the property's value. You will need to determine the market value of the property in a *repaired* condition. There are several alternatives available to you.

You can look in your local newspapers for people who are selling properties that are similar in location and style to the foreclosure property you are interested in. Visit the advertised properties and compare them to what you have chosen to bid on. You will have to compare the sizes of the lots that the houses are built on, the number and sizes of the rooms, the properties' locations, the improvements that have been added, the property taxes, the school districts, and so on. This may help you get an idea of the value of the property you wish to bid on. However, this method is not very accurate because you would be basing your value on the asking price of the people who are selling rather than on the price that someone *actually paid* for it, a price that would be significantly more accurate in the context of market value.

You can hire an appraiser and pay a fee to obtain an appraisal of the value of the property (or properties) you are interested in. You will have an accurate report of market value, but appraisals can be expensive. If you are interested in 10 or 20 properties, then appraisal costs can quickly become prohibitive, especially since you have no guarantee that you will be the successful high bidder in an auction situation, and if you are going to submit an offer through any other method, you have no guarantee that it will be accepted either. Therefore, you may have wasted the money that you spent on the appraisals.

Another available alternative is both accurate and (in most cases) free. What if I took you up in my helicopter and dropped you (gently) in a strange town? How would you find out about where you landed? About the economic makeup of the area, where the stores and schools were, what the prices and values of houses were? Your best resource is your local real estate company. Most real estate professionals are experts about the neighborhoods they work in. Will the local real estate company want to help you if they are not getting any commission? Yes, they would. Why? Because they know that, even though they may not be getting a commission this time, you (or someone you know) may need their help selling a house later on. If you're an investor, you might need them to help you rent the property to tenants, or you might use their services to buy more properties. And even if you never needed their help, you would probably recommend them to someone you know who is looking to buy or sell property because they did you a favor, they did it well, and you are grateful. Word of mouth is essential to successful real estate professionals. For these reasons, I suggest that you contact two or three real estate offices that are in the immediate area of the property you are interested in. Ask them if they can provide a comparative market analysis (real estate jargon for an informal appraisal) to give you an accurate value of the property *in a repaired condition*. They will use their resources to determine the value of your property based on the selling prices of comparable properties in the immediate area that have been sold recently.

Calculating Cash Flow

If you are an investor who intends to use your foreclosure as a rental property, or if you plan to purchase multiunit residential or commercial rental property, you will need to calculate your projected cash flow.

As briefly discussed in Chapter 8, cash flow is the money that flows into and out of a rental property. Normally the rental income, less the repairs, carrying charges, and other operating expenses, determines the cash flow for a property. Different classifications of rental property require different methods of calculating cash flow. Cash flow calculations for small investment properties, such as one-, two-, or three-family houses, will be less complicated than larger multifamily or commercial properties. Your operating costs and expenses may include maintenance fees, management costs, and other costs that are part of the daily upkeep of larger properties. Contact your accountant or financial expert about cash flow projections if you intend to purchase foreclosures for investment purposes.

Figure 9-5 details the cash flow projection for a single-family house in which the tenants are responsible for payment of all utilities and lawn-care services. In Figure 9-5, the monthly rental income must exceed the carrying charges of $1450 in order to achieve a positive cash flow. A negative cash flow will result if the rental income is less than $1450 a month. Repair expenses that exist at the time of the purchase have already been calculated as part of the cost of purchasing the property. The tenants will be paying for the monthly utilities; therefore utilities are not included as part of the carrying charges.

You will need to verify carefully that your cash flow projections and monthly expenses are accurate. Any unrealistic cash flow expectations

---

A Cash Flow Projection

Property: 123 Smith Street, Anytown, U.S.A.

Anticipated Monthly Rental Income $1,500

Monthly Mortgage Payment $1,200

Monthly Property Taxes $2,400/Yr   +   200

Monthly Property Insurance   +   50

Total Carrying Charges $1,450

Monthly Cash Flow Projection $ 50

Figure 9-5.   An example of a cash flow projection for a single-family dwelling.

relating to monthly income and carrying charges can be disastrous. For example, in Figure 9-5, let's assume a projected monthly rental income of $1500. This would yield an expected positive cash flow of $50 per month, since our carrying charges total $1450. One of the monthly expenses is the real estate property taxes that you are expecting to pay. The taxes may be lower for the present owner due to a tax exemption that you, as the new owner, are not eligible for. This includes senior citizen and veteran's property tax breaks. If you expected your property tax expense to be $200 per month because that's what the current owner is paying, but the taxes are increased to $300 monthly when you become the new owner, your positive cash flow of $50 monthly becomes a negative cash flow of $50 monthly. Another property tax snag may be in the form of separately billed taxes, such as school taxes and incorporated village taxes, which are billed in addition to the property taxes. Also remember that (surprise, surprise!) there may be improvements for which the previous owner never obtained the proper (or any, for that matter) building permits. Once you have obtained these important documents, your property taxes may increase accordingly. If you have not considered all of these taxes, then the extra expense will cause a big problem for you from day one. Most property taxes can be verified at the tax assessor's office in the town (or city) where the premises are located.

Coming up in Chapter 10, we take the information we have gathered from our inspections, the questions we asked, and the hidden expenses we uncovered, and we use it to formulate our bid sheets.

10

Preparing Your Bid Sheet

In Chapter 10 we implement the step-by-step procedures for calculating expenses and preparing a bid sheet. This process helps people organize their information, distinguish their foreclosure "wants" from their foreclosure "needs," redefine their priorities; and ultimately, avoid purchasing overpriced foreclosures.

If you have completed the preliminary research on more than one or two properties, Chapter 10 will also help you narrow down your selection of properties so that you can concentrate on those that are most worth pursuing.

Identify the Property's Condition

In Chapter 9 we divided the condition of foreclosed properties into four categories (see: *Chapter 9—The Preliminary Inspection*) in the context of *preliminary research* preparations. Now, in Chapter 10, we revisit these four conditions—this time in the context of *bid sheet* preparations.

Here are the steps to take for preparing bid sheets for foreclosed properties in each of these four conditions:

- *Vacant and accessible;* no one lives there and you can go inside and inspect.
- *Occupied and accessible;* someone lives there and you can go inside and inspect.
- *Vacant and inaccessible;* no one lives there and there is no access for you to go inside to inspect.
- *Occupied and inaccessible;* remember the angry, unfriendly occupant with the rabid pit bull and the loaded shotgun from Chapter 9?

Condition 1: Vacant and Accessible

Take the following steps to prepare bid sheets for properties that are vacant and accessible:

1. *Get prices for repairs.* Bring a licensed contractor and/or an engineer to the premises to uncover structural deficiencies and to give you a written, itemized estimate that includes the price of the repairs, and the time it will take to complete them.

2. *Determine the market value of the property in a repaired condition.* As explained in Chapter 9, you can estimate the value of a property by conducting your own research, by obtaining a professional appraisal, or by consulting with the real estate professionals in the neighborhoods that are of interest to you. If you intend to rent the property out to tenants, you must also obtain estimates for rental income in order to prepare your cash flow analysis.

3. *Calculate your bid limits.* Generally, the market value of the property in a repaired condition, less the expenses and repairs required during and after the purchase, gives you a pretty accurate guideline of the price to pay for a break-even transaction. Once you have established the break-even point, you can make adjustments and prepare offers in accordance with your individual goals.

Figure 10-1 is an illustration of a Bid-Calculating Worksheet to help you organize your computations.

Figure 10-1 was created for the purpose of purchasing a foreclosure at an auction, and may also be used for preparing other kinds of offers. Figure 10-1 illustrates how the information we acquired during our preliminary preparations is applied to the bid sheet in order to calculate our bid limits accurately. In our example, the opening bid amount, or asking price, is $60,000. We have estimated the property's market value in a repaired condition to be $100,000. If the property is being purchased as an investment property to rent out to others, we will need to estimate the expected monthly rental income. In this case, the projected monthly rental income is $800.

Next, we estimate our expenses; those that will be incurred before, during, and after the closing. The expenses that are usually incurred before and at the time of the closing are those that are usually associated with the purchase itself, (i.e., insurance policies, mortgage financing, closing costs, property documents, utility expenses, unpaid taxes, etc.). Expenses that are usually incurred after the closing include repair costs, eviction expenses, and the cost of rent loss. In Figure 10-1, we have estimated our insurance costs (including title insurance and property insurance) to be $1000. There are no mortgage costs included because we are purchasing the property with cash; therefore, no mortgage loan is needed. We have estimated our repair expenses to be $10,000, based on estimates from our contractor and engineer. Our contractor estimated that it would take one month to complete the repairs; therefore, we must include a

BID-CALCULATING WORKSHEET

Opening Bid Amount: $ 60,000

Estimated Market Value Repaired: $100,000

Anticipated Monthly Rental Income: $ 800

Expenses:

Estimated Insurance: $ 1,000

Estimated Mortgage Cost:

Estimated Closing Cost:

Property Document Cost:

Utility Expenses:

Repair Costs: $10,000

Eviction Costs:

Unpaid Taxes: $ 200 ($2,400/year for 30 days)

Anticipated Rent Loss: $ 800 (For 1 month during repairs)

Other Expenses:

Total Expenses: $12,000

Estimated Market Value: $100,000

Deduct Expenses: −$ 12,000

Amount to Bid for a Break-Even Purchase: **$ 88,000**

Figure 10-1. Bid-calculating worksheet.

rent-loss expense of $800 in our calculations. We have confirmed that the unpaid property taxes total $200 for the 30 days between the contract and the closing, based on the property tax amount of $2400 a year. Our total expenses add up to $12,000.

We have estimated the market value of the property in a repaired condition to be $100,000. From this number, we deduct $12,000 for expenses, which gives us our amount to bid for a "break-even purchase price" of $88,000. If the auction contract terms require a 10-percent down payment from the successful high bidder, we would bring $8800 with us to the auction. Right? Good.

But wait a moment...did we just say that we are buying a property for $88,000 and spending another $12,000 on repairs, and the property is *only* going to be worth $100,000? Why don't we just buy a traditional resale for $100,000 and save ourselves a lot of extra work?

Well, $88,000 is *just* the break-even price—the price we would offer if we expected to pay full market price (i.e., one dollar on the dollar). Once we have established the break-even price, we can adjust our offers according to our goals. For example, someone who wants to buy the house to live in and raise a family may be better off paying one dollar on the dollar now, and waiting to collect a profit after the property is sold, in years to come. For this buyer, the primary goal is a long-term home. By contrast, the primary goal for investors and profit-oriented buyers is a discounted purchase price. On the average, these kinds of buyers limit their purchases to 75 percent of our $100,000 value (i.e., 75 cents on the dollar) or $75,000 as a starting point, from which we deduct our $12,000 expenses. So, in our example, we end up with a maximum bid limit of $63,000. Using the aforementioned 10-percent down payment requirement as a guide, we bring $6300 with us to the auction as our down payment, in case we are the high bidder.

Applying investing principles, I know some investors who purchase foreclosures at auctions and who would bring one certified check for $6000 and *three* certified checks for $100 each. The checks are all made payable to their own names. If they are the high bidders for less than the $63,000 limit they set, let's say $61,000, they only have to give $6100 as the down payment, and can redeposit the remaining $200 back into their bank accounts! I said they were investors, right? Remember, investors do not like to tie up their own money if they don't have to.

Sometimes a buyer at an auction bids much higher than we would have. It is possible that the buyer either overestimated the property value or underestimated the expenses. On the other hand, the buyer may be a contractor, who already has the material he needs (that would have cost us $10,000) stored in his or her garage. If such is the case, that contractor can bid higher—and has a better chance of getting the property—than someone who does not have the same advantage. The same thing may hold true in a situation where there are anticipated legal fees and the bidder is a real estate attorney who will get the benefit of lower legal fees than the next bidder.

The process of preparing your bid sheet not only helps you calculate your final bidding price, it also prevents you from being caught up in "auction fever"—a situation where the competitive atmosphere overcomes your common sense and you keep bidding <u>even after</u> the price exceeds the property value. How does your bid sheet prevent this craziness? Because you only bring enough money with you to cover the required down payment—10 percent of your bid sheet calculations—so the maximum amount you can bid up to is limited to the price limit you set for yourself when you were sane.

You can use this same bid calculating worksheet to prepare your written offers for REO properties, and to purchase homes from delinquent borrowers. Financing fees and mortgage loan expenses can range significantly from state to state, and you should consult with experts in your state (i.e., your attorney, your financial advisor, your accountant, your lender, etc.) to make sure that you have taken all of your expenses into consideration.

Condition 2: Occupied and Accessible

In this situation, the occupants allow you to enter the property. You will therefore have an opportunity to view the property and meet the occupants. Take the following steps to prepare bid sheets for properties that are occupied and accessible:

1. *Obtain estimates for repairs.* Bring your contractor or engineer and get reports and estimates of repairs including the length of time for completion. You can ask the occupants about any structural or appliance defects, or problems they are having with plumbing, heating, and electrical systems.

2. *Inquire about the present occupant's preference regarding continued occupancy.* The occupants are either the delinquent homeowners or their tenants. Sometimes the tenants are in shock when you show up to inspect the property. They have been paying their rent each month and had no idea that the landlord was not paying the mortgage. Sometimes, however, *it is* the tenants who are causing the foreclosure—by *not* paying their rent.

If the occupants are tenants of the delinquent owners and you intend to rent out the property if you are the successful bidder, you may want to offer the tenants a new lease with you. Most state laws provide that, as long as there was proper service of the legal documents when the foreclosure action began, the new owner is not bound by the tenant's lease with the delinquent homeowner, because leases are subordinate to mortgages. Ask your attorney whether this is the case in your state. You are also not responsible for refunds of any security deposits that the tenants may have given the previous owner, and the tenants should be aware that they must look to the previous owner for reimbursement.

If you expect to live there yourself and wish to have the occupants evicted, or if the occupants seem undesirable (i.e., one hint may be the five cars dissembled on the front lawn) and you want them to leave, you can add eviction expenses to your bid calculations.

If the occupants were the previous owners, you may wish to negotiate rental terms with them should you become the new owner. If negotiated, you would allow them to stay in the property under the terms of a new lease with you. One property I inspected was occupied by the delinquent owners who were being foreclosed on. They had kept the place in excellent condition and wanted to know if I would let them stay if I were the successful bidder. Their son was about to begin his last year in high school, and they didn't want to move until after his graduation. They had been very helpful and accommodating, and they let me inspect the property several times. These people were good potential tenants. They kept the place clean and in good condition, they were highly motivated to continue to live there as tenants, and they would be very conscientious about paying their rent on time in order to remain there. Also, the fact that someone is being foreclosed on does not always eliminate that person as a candidate for renting the property. While it may be true that they could not afford the $1200 first mortgage and the $1500 second mortgage on the property when they were the owners, they most likely can afford the $1500 per month for rent that you would be charging them.

3. *Calculate your bid limits.* Calculate your bid sheet in the same manner as when the property was vacant but accessible, but if there is an anticipated eviction looming in the horizon, the costs of it must be added to your expenses. Also remember to include the cost of lost rent that may be incurred during the eviction proceedings. Contact an attorney with experience in performing legal evictions for a more accurate estimate of these costs.

Condition 3: Vacant and Inaccessible

This is the <u>*least desirable*</u> condition in foreclosure bidding. In this situation, you are bidding on a property that you are unable to inspect. Sometimes access is denied as an administrative requirement by the insurance policy carrier, and sometimes access is denied because the house has so much structural damage (i.e., floors or ceilings that are caving in) that it would be dangerous to allow people in to inspect it.

You could be bidding on a property that could be a complete disaster. Even if the property looks okay on the outside, there is absolutely no guarantee that the inside is in good condition. I have encountered collapsed cesspools, polluted wells, sewer hookups that are only partially completed, broken pipes, frozen pipes, no pipes. It almost seemed as though the people who were foreclosed on said to themselves, "If I can't have this house, then neither can anyone else!"

Your repair costs may equal or exceed the purchase price. This is not a recommended situation for someone who is new at purchasing foreclosures. Preparing a bid sheet is difficult when you cannot determine your repair expenses, and a mistaken "guesstimate" can cost thousands of dollars.

Most lenders will not approve a mortgage loan if the bank appraiser is unable to get access to the inside of the premises to check that the plumbing, heating, and electric systems are in good working order, or if there are major structural repairs that need to be completed. Buying a property that you cannot inspect first is like buying a car without looking under the hood. Unless you are very handy and can afford to make repairs at minimum costs, or plan to knock the structure down completely and rebuild from scratch, avoid foreclosures that are vacant and inaccessible. Move on and look for a different property where you *can* get inside to inspect.

Condition 4: Occupied and Inaccessible

Properties that are occupied but inaccessible are also very risky. You may be encountering bitter, unfriendly people who refuse to cooperate and won't allow you into the house to inspect it before you bid. In such situations, I was able to gain access to the house by sympathizing with the people who reside there. Sometimes, if the occupants appeared to be taking good care of the property and I intended to rent the property to tenants anyway, I offered them the opportunity to remain there under a new lease with me if I was the high bidder.

CHECKLIST: PRIOR TO BIDDING

❑ Determine the "purchase price" range that best reflects your current financial situation and your future goals.

❑ Ask the "prebid" questions.

❑ Inspect the premises.

❑ Research the status of missing documents (i.e., survey, Certificate of Occupancy, etc.).

❑ Get a written estimate for repairs from a licensed contractor and/or engineer.

❑ Inspect the file of the foreclosure action (if possible).

❑ Determine the market value of the property in a repaired condition.

❑ Determine the rental value, if applicable.

❑ Calculate expenses.

❑ Consider the status of current occupants (if applicable).

❑ Research eviction fees and the time for completion (if necessary).

❑ Calculate your bid limits on a bid sheet.

❑ Contact the referee or foreclosing lender's attorney to confirm the final upset price.

❑ Contact the referee or foreclosing lender's attorney to confirm that the auction is still on.

Please Note: Not All-Inclusive—Additional Information May Be Required.

Figure 10-2. Sample checklist: prior to bidding.

In the event that you wish to move into the property yourself, or if you do not wish to offer the current occupants a lease for any reason, I found it very effective to offer *moving money* (dollar compensation also known as "cash for keys") to pay the costs of moving expenses for the occupants. Do we just whip out our wallets and pay them? Of course not! We haven't even gone to the auction yet. We sign an agreement that *if* we are the successful high bidders, we will pay the occupants *after* we own the property, *after* they have removed all of their belongings out, and *if* the premises are left in broom-clean and good condition. Money is only given to the occupants *after* they have fulfilled their end of the agreement, moved out, and turned the keys over to you. Money is a very effective tool to offer to offset the inconvenience of moving and as an incentive for potentially hostile occupants to leave both quickly and peacefully. At any rate, *extreme caution* is urged if you wish to buy a foreclosure under these circumstances. The potential risks are obvious, and may be costly because you will be dealing with unfriendly occupants who are in a position to cause significant damage to the property. It may not be worth the time or money you would be expending.

Final Confirmation

Two final preliminary preparations are suggested. The first concerns bidding at an auction, the second concerns mailing in a written offer.

Before bidding on a foreclosure at an auction, you should contact the referee or designated authority to confirm that the sale is still on, and that the delinquent homeowners have not gotten an extension or exercised their right of redemption by paying all the arrears. Also confirm the final opening bid amount. Sometimes the opening bid will be higher than the amount that was originally published, due to additional legal fees or other expenses.

Lastly, in the event that you are submitting your bid to purchase a foreclosure through a written offer, be sure to follow up on the status of your offer daily until you know whether it has been accepted or rejected.

An example of a checklist for use prior to bidding is included as Figure 10-2. The checklist combines the preliminary research preparations from Chapter 9 with the preliminary bid sheet preparations from Chapter 10.

11

Congratulations! You Are the Successful High Bidder

Once your offer or bid is accepted, you can hit the ground running if you have a plan of action and procedures in place to help you complete the transaction.

In Chapter 11, we review the procedures to follow for purchasing foreclosures when (1) you are the high bidder at an auction; (2) your offer for a bank-owned or government-owned property has been accepted by the seller; and/or (3) you have successfully negotiated the price and terms for a preauction foreclosure with the delinquent homeowner.

When You Are the High Bidder at the Auction...

When you are the successful high bidder at an auction and you are awarded the sales contract, your first priority is to organize the final closing arrangements. This is because time is usually of the essence; many mortgage foreclosure auctions require a 30-day closing, which leaves you with a lot to accomplish in an abbreviated time frame. The paperwork you receive from the referee should document the terms of the sale, including the date you are expected to close, the amount you gave as your down payment, and the remaining balance due at closing. Verify all of your prebid questions, including repair responsibility and costs, insurance requirements, occupancy status, and the availability of property documents (i.e., Torrens title, certificate of occupancy, survey, and so on). If you have not already done so, you should contact your attorney, financial advisor, and any other professionals who will be assisting you in completing your purchase. If you are purchasing the foreclosure with cash, confirm the final amount you will need for your closing costs. If you have taken steps to obtain financing from a lending institution (i.e., received a preapproval), contact your attorney and/or financial advisor to ask about the next steps to take to prepare for the closing, now that you have a contract from the referee.

When Your Offer for a
Bank- or Government-Owned
Foreclosure Is Accepted...

After your offer is accepted by a bank or a government agency and the contract documents are issued, your attorney should examine the terms of the sale and explain the rest of the process to you so that you know what to expect. If you are buying the foreclosure with cash, confirm the accuracy of your closing cost calculations with your attorney and/or financial advisor. If the bank or government agency that accepted your offer is providing the financing for the foreclosure, your attorney should verify and explain the terms, conditions, and closing costs.

When Your Offer to
the Delinquent Owner
Is Accepted...

After the delinquent owner accepts your offer, arrange to get your agreement in writing. Depending on the custom in your area, one of the parties (or his or her attorney) will prepare the sales contract with the terms and conditions that the buyer and seller agreed to. If the delinquent owner provides the contract, review it carefully to ensure that the terms stipulated in the contract are in accordance with your expectations, based on the agreement that you made with the seller. Your attorney will order a title report to ensure that there are no additional liens or judgments. Your attorney should also verify any financing terms you arranged with the foreclosing lender. For example, if you arranged to assume the delinquent owner's outstanding mortgage balance, your attorney should finalize the assumption terms. If you will be obtaining financing from another source, your attorney and the lending institution's representative should assist in preparing you for the closing.

Unlike auctions and bank or government foreclosure sales where you are purchasing the premises in an "as-is" condition, you have more negotiating power when it comes to the sales terms in a preauction purchase because you are negotiating directly with the owners who are in control of the personal and real property that they are selling you. For example, your contract negotiations should address the specific fixtures and appliances that are included in the sale, and should describe them in detail. (Taking photos is also highly recommended.) Does the sale include the air conditioner that was installed in the living room wall? How about the one in the master bedroom window? Which refrigerator is staying with the house; the new frost-free model with the external ice water/ice cube dispenser, or the 1960 model stored in the basement? Don't forget landscaping; will the seller be leaving all of the shrubs, trees, and plants? Are the expensive window treatments and decorative doorknobs included in the sale? The closing date, lead paint disclosures, and property condition disclosures (if applicable), lease terms (if tenants are currently occupying the premises), vacating terms (if or when the delinquent owners or their tenants will be moving out), security refunds (if applicable), and so on, should also be included as part of the contract agreement.

Coast to the Closing with These Five Standard Operating Procedures

These *Standard Operating Procedures* can help you organize your priorities and eliminate closing delays.

Standard Operating Procedure 1: Order Your Appropriate Insurance

Prior to the closing, if you have not already done so when you executed the sales contract, you will have to purchase a property insurance policy. If you will be living in the premises, you will need a homeowner's insurance policy (for an owner-occupied dwelling). If you will be renting the property out to tenants, you will need a landlord's policy (for a non-owner-occupied dwelling). Contact your insurance agent to discuss the best rates and terms for your individual needs. To avoid any lapse in insurance coverage for your foreclosure, you are required to provide a prepaid property insurance policy that is in effect on the day you take title as the new owner.

Standard Operating Procedure 2: Protect the Premises

If the property is vacant, confirm that it has been secured in a manner that prevents trespasser intrusion. Most insurance companies will either arrange to have vacant houses boarded up by their own contractors, or they will provide the owner with the requisite board-up specifications, which the owner can pass along to his or her own contractors. If the foreclosing lender is responsible for the care and protection of the premises until the closing, you should document the condition of the property *immediately*, including signed and dated pictures, video tape, and witnesses.

If there were 12 unbroken windows in the house when you were the high bidder, then there should be 12 unbroken windows when you close on the property. If the property was boarded up, doors and windows were most likely removed first. You should request information about the location of those windows and doors. The foreclosing lender's insurance should cover any damages. Another option is to have an alarm system installed that is monitored 24 hours a day, 7 days a week by a central station operator who can ensure that the police (and you) are notified if the alarm becomes activated.

If the property is occupied, your contract with the lending institution probably stipulates that (aside from casualty such as fire or smoke damage) they will not be responsible for any cosmetic damages to the premises caused by the occupants. In most cases, any repairs that will be needed after you close will be your responsibility in this situation.

Standard Operating Procedure 3:
Hire a Neighbor

Visit the next-door neighbors and express your concern for the safety of your new purchase. Since you will be making improvements to what may be considered the neighborhood "eyesore," the neighbors are likely to be extremely cooperative. Try to find that omnipresent, ever-watchful neighbor who knows at every moment exactly what's going on in every house in the neighborhood. Pay him or her to put this natural talent to good use. Offer a fee for house-watching services that simply involves notifying you, or the police, of any break-ins or other disturbances. Provide a contact number so this person can reach you in case there are problems.

In houses that are set far apart from any neighbors, some people can be quite creative. One investor told me about a technique he used to discourage break-ins, where, if one of his properties was vacant, he posted a sign with a skull and crossbones on the front door that read, "**Danger! Poison Gas Leak**" in large letters. No one ever broke into his houses! This example was just for illustration purposes, and is not recommended as a remedy—your neighbors are likely to freak out if they walk out their front doors and see a warning like that posted on a house that is just 20 feet away!

Standard Operating Procedure 4:
Order a Title Search and Title
Insurance

Under no circumstances should you take a chance on closing without first obtaining the title report and title insurance. The purpose of ordering the title report and title insurance is to help you uncover any existing liens or judgments currently attached to the property. While in most cases, property that is bank-owned or owned by a government agency will have clear title, there is no guarantee to that effect. The title report is particularly valuable to a preauction purchaser because it can uncover the third mortgage on the property that the delinquent owner "forgot" to disclose to you, and that you as the new owner would have been responsible for.

The title report would also reveal private land-use restrictions or encumbrances that could render the property difficult or impossible to sell in the future.

One other option that many purchasers find especially valuable is to have the title company "insure the survey" in order to verify that it is an accurate illustration of the property's legal description and dimensions.

Standard Operating Procedure 5: Apply for Your Financing (if Applicable)

If you have purchased a property at an auction that requires a strict closing date (such as 30 days), or signed a contract with a "time is of the essence" closing date that is within 30 or even 60 days, hopefully you have expedited the mortgage procedure by getting preapproved for a mortgage loan before you bid on any properties. (See Chapter 9—*Prequalified versus Preapproved.*) During the mortgage processing procedure, you can further expedite the loan approval by providing bank personnel or appraisers with access to inspect the property as quickly as possible. Remember, financing may be delayed if the premises are occupied by unfriendly occupants who won't allow the lending institution's representatives inside to perform their inspections. Delays may also occur if the structure or systems need major repairs. The risk here is that you could lose your down payment. Unless you can come up with the balance of your purchase price in cash, You may need to secure interim financing to close with. Have your attorney review your agreement to ensure that you understand all the conditions that you are expected to comply with.

In cases where the REO seller is providing you with financing for the property that you are purchasing from its inventory, closing rules may vary from one REO seller to the next. Your attorney can help advise you about the specific conditions that apply in your situation.

If you have purchased your foreclosure from a government agency (HUD, DVA, GSA, FDIC, etc.), and the agency is also providing you with financing, you should confirm the financing and closing procedures. Have your attorney review your paperwork so that you are familiar with your specific role and responsibilities. Again, your cooperation in response to any requests for additional information from the lender will expedite the loan approval process significantly.

Applying the Five Standard Operating Procedures to Your Particular Circumstances

Once your offer has been accepted, and your contract is executed, you can apply the *Standard Operating Procedures* to each of the four property conditions enumerated in Chapter 9 (in the context of preliminary research preparations), and in Chapter 10 (in the context of bid sheet preparations). In Chapter 11, we revisit the four conditions once again— this time in the context of "after-contract preparations." Let's go through these procedures now, in a step-by-step fashion.

After Contract: Implementing the Standard Operating Procedures for Vacant and Accessible Foreclosures

1. *Follow the five Standard Operating Procedures.*

2. *Get your rental permit.* If you intend to rent the property to tenants, and a rental permit is required, contact the building department, or other appropriate agency, and begin the procedure to obtain this document.

3. *Market the property.* If you intend to market the property for sale or rent, and the repairs needed are negligible, begin your advertising now. Once a tenant has been found, a lease or rental agreement can be negotiated and prepared for signature. Be sensitive to the fact that once you close, you lose money every day that the premises are vacant. Therefore, if the tenant can take possession on the day you close, this will ensure you of immediate rental income.

After Contract: Implementing the Standard Operating Procedures for Occupied and Accessible Foreclosures

1. *Follow the five Standard Operating Procedures.*

2. *Contact the occupants.* Send what I call a "greetings" letter both by certified and first-class mail. The first-class letter is sent as a courtesy; that is, if the occupants are unable to go to the post office to pick up the certified letter, they will still receive your notification via first-class mail. The occupants that you are addressing in this letter were cooperative and allowed you to inspect the property before you bid on it or made your offer to purchase it. When the occupants receive your letter and contact you, any agreements you made during your previous inspections can now be finalized.

Figure 11-1 is a sample greetings letter sent to cooperative occupants. Use this letter when:

- You have acquired the property at an auction and the property is occupied by either the delinquent homeowners or their tenant(s).
- You purchased the property as a result of negotiations with the delinquent homeowners, and the occupants are their tenant(s).
- The property is an REO, and the occupants are either the previous homeowners who were foreclosed on or their tenant(s).
- You have purchased the property from a government agency, and the occupants are the previous homeowners or their tenant(s).

3. *If the occupants will be renting the premises from you,* you can have a lease or rental agreement prepared and ready to sign on the day you close. Let the occupants preview the lease so that any problems can be resolved in advance. Remind them (if applicable) that they must look to their previous landlord for any security refunds that are due them under their old lease, and provide them with the details about the security deposit they will need when they sign the new lease with you.

4. *If the occupants will be repurchasing the property from you,* a sales contract should be drawn up with the terms of your agreement.

5. *If the occupants will be moving out,* you should organize this arrangement so that you are aware of, and therefore in better control of, the vacating procedure. You will need to know the date that the occupants will be moving out so you can arrange to be there to collect the keys and to secure the premises.

After Contract: Implementing the Standard Operating Procedures for Vacant and Inaccessible Foreclosures

1. *Follow the five standard operating procedures.*

2. *Continue to inspect the premises on a regular basis.* If vandalism occurs, inform the designated authority so that proper insurance procedures can be followed.

3. *If you have taken possession of the property and are responsible for any damages,* you will need to advise your own insurance agency about any claims.

After Contract: Implementing the Standard Operating Procedures for Occupied and Inaccessible Foreclosures

1. *Follow the five standard operating procedures.*

GREETINGS LETTER—SENT TO COOPERATIVE OCCUPANTS

(Send Via Certified Mail—Return Receipt Requested, and First Class)

Today's Date:

Dear _____:
      (Occupant's Name)

This is to advise you that I have purchased the property that you are occupying (at an auction I attended)/(from the bank)/(from the government agency) on _____.
                           (Date of Auction/Contract)

I have been advised that you are still occupying the property and that you may be interested in arranging (purchase)/(rental) terms with me.

Please contact the undersigned at your earliest convenience to discuss this matter further.

My telephone number is (   ) _____.
                         (Area Code and Telephone Number)

The best time to reach me is _____.
                       (Day and Time)

Very truly yours,

_____
     (Your Signature)

Figure 11-1. An example of a "greetings" letter to cooperative occupants.

2. *Contact the occupants.* Send a "greetings" letter to the occupants. Unlike the greetings letter sent to the cooperative occupants, this letter is being sent to occupants who *did not* cooperate with you during your initial attempt to gain access to the premises. Any response you receive from these occupants will help determine your next move—eviction, a new lease, or moving money. Use the same mailing protocol for uncooperative occupants as for cooperative occupants (i.e., send the greetings letter both certified and first class).

Figure 11-2 is a sample greetings letter to uncooperative occupants. Use this letter when:

- Your attempts to contact the occupants have been unsuccessful.
- The occupants have not responded to previous requests to contact you and you will be initiating legal eviction procedures to get them out. If the eviction laws in your state require tenant notification prior to initiating an eviction proceeding, you can produce the certified letter that was returned to you undelivered by the post office as evidence that you attempted to communicate with the occupants.
- You want to get the occupants' attention by offering moving money in return for their cooperation.

3. *If the occupants ask about renting the premises from you,* and you want to consider them as potential tenants, you can have a lease or rental agreement prepared and ready to sign on the day you close. Same as with the cooperative occupants, let the occupants preview the lease so that any problems can be resolved and questions answered in advance. Remind them (if applicable) that they must look to their previous landlord for any security refunds that are due them under their old lease, and provide them with the details about the security deposit that they will need when they sign a new lease with you.

4. *If the occupants wish to repurchase the property from you,* a contract could be negotiated and drawn up with the terms of your agreement.

5. *If the occupants will be moving out,* you should organize this arrangement so that you are aware of, and therefore in control of, the vacating procedure. You will have to draw up an agreement with the terms that you have agreed to, including the amount of money you will pay, and the conditions that the occupants must meet in return for the payment.

An After-Contract Checklist

Figure 11-3 is a basic checklist of things to be done after the contract has been signed. This checklist is not intended to be all-inclusive.

<u>GREETINGS LETTER—SENT TO UNCOOPERATIVE OCCUPANTS</u>

(Send Via Certified Mail—Return Receipt Requested, and First Class)

Today's Date:

Dear _____:
        (Occupant's Name)

This is to advise you that I have purchased the property that you are occupying (at an auction I attended)/(from the bank)/(from the government agency) on _____.
                    (Date of Auction/Contract)

I have been advised that you are still occupying the property, and I would appreciate it if you could contact me concerning your plans to move out. I understand the inconvenience that this may cause and would like to discuss financial assistance that I may be able to offer you towards moving costs or other expenses.

Please contact the undersigned at your earliest convenience to discuss this matter further.

My telephone number is (   ) _____.
                            (Area Code and Telephone Number)

The best time to reach me is _____.
                      (Day and Time)

Very truly yours,

_____
(Your Signature)

Figure 11-2. An example of a "greetings" letter to uncooperative occupants.

AFTER THE CONTRACT IS SIGNED, DO THE FOLLOWING:

( ) Order the appropriate property insurance.

( ) Take pictures of the property to preserve a record of the condition.

( ) Protect the premises.

( ) Hire a neighbor.

( ) Order a title search and title insurance.

( ) Apply for a mortgage loan (if applicable).

( ) Obtain a rental permit (if required).

( ) Market the property (if desired).

( ) Send out greetings letters (if necessary).

( ) Organize vacancy arrangements with occupants (if applicable).

Please Note—Not All-Inclusive—Additional Information May Be Required

Figure 11-3. Sample checklist: After the contract.

12

Now That You Own the Property

After you close on your foreclosure and are the proud new owner, you still have a few more steps to take. So, pat yourself on the back and follow along to complete the transaction.

Steps to Take for Completing the Transaction

Record the Closing Documents

Your attorney should make certain that your closing documents are properly recorded. If you are not represented by an attorney, the person who customarily is charged with bringing the applicable documents (deed, financing documents, etc.) to the recording office will be providing that service for you.

Schedule the Repair Work

If you will be completing repair work yourself, or you are hiring a licensed contractor, you can begin the repairs on your foreclosure after you close. If you are planning to use the property as an investment that will be rented out to others, and the property is vacant now, it is important that repairs be made as expeditiously as possible in order to avoid costly rent losses. (Chapter 13 covers procedures for making repairs to your foreclosure.)

Restore the Utility Services

If your foreclosure is currently vacant and in need of repairs, the utilities (water, gas, electric) should be turned on so that work can begin quickly.

If the utilities are in the previous owner's name, as in an REO or government foreclosure purchase, have them transferred to your name to avoid service interruptions. If you have tenants moving in and your rental agreement stipulates that they will be responsible for utility services, advise them to contact the utility companies to have service transferred to their names before they move in. (The utility companies may require a deposit fee from your tenants if they are new customers.)

Begin Eviction Proceedings (if Applicable)

Depending on the legal requirement in your state, the eviction of any occupants living in the premises may be delayed until the deed has been recorded in the town or county clerk's office. If there is a recording backlog and the deed cannot be recorded for a long period of time, this could delay the eviction procedure. Your attorney should be consulted for the proper procedure to follow. The recording office personnel may also be able to give you some suggestions on how to expedite this procedure.

Contact Your Local Tax Collector

Contact the tax collector's office in the town where your new property is located and let them know of your new ownership. If you have obtained or assumed a mortgage with an escrow for property taxes, the lender collects the taxes as part of your monthly mortgage payment, and will be responsible for forwarding payments directly to the tax collector in a timely manner. On the other hand, if you have purchased your foreclosure with cash, or if the lender does not escrow for real estate property taxes, you will be responsible for payment of the property taxes directly to the tax collector.

Once the deed showing you as the new owner is recorded, the tax collector will have notice of your new ownership and can forward the new tax bills to you. If, however, there is a backlog in the recording office, there may be delays in sending you the new tax bills. This could result in penalties charged to you for late payments.

To help prevent unnecessary delays with your property tax bill, send a letter to the tax collector's office identifying yourself as the new owner. Include the property description of your foreclosure to help the tax collector identify your property correctly. Send the letter by certified mail and request that all future tax bills be sent to you at the appropriate address for payment. In the event that late charges or penalties accrue because of the tax collector's failure to send you the notices, you may be

AFTER THE CLOSING, DO THE FOLLOWING:

( ) Closing documents should be recorded, as required.

( ) Begin necessary repair work.

( ) Restore utility services.

( ) Begin eviction proceedings (if required).

( ) Advise the tax collector(s) of your new ownership.

( ) Execute the lease with your tenants (if applicable).

Not All-Inclusive—Additional Information May Be Required

Figure 12-1. Sample checklist: After the closing.

able to have the penalties abated since you can prove that you notified the proper authorities of your new ownership. Make certain to send a letter to each party that will receive tax payments, including school, town, and village tax collectors.

Execute the Lease

If you have arranged for tenants to rent the property, you can now execute the lease or rental agreement with them. It is helpful to review all the terms of the lease or rental agreement with your tenants. Make certain that the tenants are aware of the date the rent is due and where it should be sent each month. Confirm the move-in date and the amount of the security deposit you will be collecting. If the tenants are already occupying the property because they were the tenants of the previous owners, or if the previous owners are going to remain there as your tenants under new lease terms with you, then a new lease agreement should be executed and a new security deposit collected.

After-Closing Checklist

Figure 12-1 is a basic checklist of things to be done after the closing has taken place. It is not intended to be all-inclusive.

13

Making Repairs to Your Foreclosure

Foreclosures are indicative of a distressed situation. People who are experiencing financial difficulties cannot afford to keep their property in prime condition. Therefore, the foreclosure you purchase may require extensive structural and/or cosmetic repairs. If you are the kind of person who thinks a "square" is a skinny guy with glasses who prefers reading books to playing sports, and that a "wood plane" is something people utilized to navigate the skies in the early 1900s, then <u>do not</u> attempt to do your own repairs. Instead, you should consider hiring a contractor to work on your foreclosure.

In Chapter 13, we combine a "competitive bidding system" with a "payment for performance initiative" so that you can begin making repairs to your foreclosure.

Pinpointing Priorities

During the years that I worked as a residential property manager, one of my responsibilities was to hire contractors to repair and/or renovate investment properties. To accomplish this task with efficiency and cost-effectiveness, a procedure was implemented that combined a "competitive bidding system" with a "payment for performance initiative." It was successful because it satisfied the needs of both parties: the property owners, whose priorities were (a) to have a professional quality of work completed (b) for a fair price and (c) in a timely fashion; and the contractors, who wanted (a) to perform work that was clearly defined in a formal agreement, and (b) to be paid for completing that work on a steady basis, as the work progressed.

Finding a Contractor

If you hired an engineer to give you a report on the property before you purchased it, the engineer may be able to recommend a contractor. Or you can ask friends, co-workers, and neighbors who had work done on their homes recently, to recommend a contractor that they were happy with. Another way to find a contractor is to look around your neighborhood for houses where contracting work is in progress. If you are unable to find contractors through these sources, you can contact companies that advertise in local newspapers or the telephone directory.

Implementing a Competitive Bidding System

Conducting the Initial Interview

For extensive renovation work, I recommend that you establish a competitive bidding system. This involves interviewing and obtaining estimates from three to five contractors and will help to ensure that you have a wider range of experienced professionals and prices to choose from. A competitive bidding system also encourages contractors to give you their best prices because they know that other contractors will be giving you prices as well. The following questions can help you gauge the knowledge and experience of the contractors.

Is the contractor licensed? Many states have licensing requirements for contractors who perform work on residential and commercial buildings within the state. Check with your local Department of Consumer Affairs to find out if licensing requirements have been adopted for contractors in your state. If so, ask if the agency can provide information concerning any complaints that have been filed against the contractors that you are obtaining bids from.

Is the contractor insured? In the event that the contractor or the contractor's employees have an accident or are injured while they are working on your property, the contractor should carry worker's compensation and liability insurance coverage for himself and his employees. Many contractors also purchase insurance policies to protect their tools and their equipment.

How long has the contractor been in business? There really is no substitute for skill and experience. Contractors who have been in business for a long period of time have had a chance to learn the best, quickest, and most efficient ways to perform their work.

Has the contractor performed work similar to the work you want done? Contractors that may be experienced in one facet of home improvements, such as roofing, may not have a great deal of experience in other areas, such as installing sheetrock and painting. Although they may be willing to try to do the work for you, you would be better off finding contractors who have experience with the specific repairs that you require.

Can you visit the contractor's current job site to look at the work in progress? If the contractor is currently working on someone else's property, you can learn a lot by visiting the premises and seeing the quality of the contractor's workmanship for yourself. If possible, ask the homeowner about the contractor's work habits, reliability, and professionalism. Is the contractor complying with the time frame and prices that he or she and the homeowner originally agreed to? Has the contractor asked the homeowner for extra money even though the homeowner hasn't asked for extra work? (It is also a good idea to ask the homeowner if the contractor is a relative. If so, there is a strong likelihood that the homeowner's opinion is somewhat biased.)

Can the contractor provide a current credit report? A credit report will have information about the contractor's financial position and will include claims or judgments from previous customers or unpaid suppliers against the contractor's company, or against him or her individually.

In cases where extensive renovation work is planned and thousands of dollars are at stake, you may want to consider establishing an escrow account with your attorney acting as the escrow agent. Here is how it works. The property owner deposits money into the escrow account in contractually agreed increments to ensure that the finances to pay for the work will be available for the contractor. Upon written notification by the homeowner that the work is complete and the conditions for releasing the funds have been met, the attorney releases the funds to the contractor from the account.

Will the contractor be hiring subcontractors? The contractor you hire may not be experienced in all of the areas of repair that you need, and will therefore hire subcontractors for this purpose. You have no control over the subcontractors that the contractor hires; however, you can certainly inquire about their level of experience, and ask for proof that they are licensed and insured.

Preparing the Bid Package for Estimates

The Specifications No matter how skilled a contractor is, the homeowner will not be satisfied if the work is not performed to his or her specifications, and it is my experience that even the best, most reputable contractors are not mind readers. For this reason, it is in the best interests of both parties for the homeowner to communicate his or her specific needs by providing the contractor with a clear description of the work the homeowner wants the contractor to do.

In order to accomplish this, the homeowner fills out a *bid specification worksheet,* which is an itemized list of the specific work that the homeowner wants the contractors to provide prices for. The bid specifications are prepared on a room-by-room basis—each room having its own page. This means that a property owner who wants renovation work completed in all three bedrooms in his or her three-bedroom house would prepare bid specifications *for each* of the three bedrooms. Similarly, if work is also required in two bathrooms, the property owner prepares two "bathroom" bid specification worksheets, one for each bathroom, etc.

A bid specification worksheet has two components—a place to list/describe the work (for the property owner to fill out); and a column for the price (for the contractor to fill out). If the homeowner is uncertain as to what structural repairs are needed, he or she can ask the contractors, who are bidding on the work, for their recommendations based on their knowledge and experience.

On major reconstruction projects, if a more detailed analysis is required, the homeowner can hire a structural engineer who specializes in residential property to prepare a report.

It is sometimes a little tricky for the contractors to distinguish one room from another—especially in a vacant house where there are several bedrooms that are similar in size and dimension. We do not want to identify the rooms by the existing colors if we are going to repaint, or for that matter, by the existing floor coverings if we are going to recarpet. I have found it helpful to assign a number to similar rooms in the house. You can thumbtack a piece of paper on the doorways with the words "bathroom #1," "bathroom #2," "bedroom #1," "bedroom #2," and "bedroom #3," etc.

The bid specification worksheets should correspond with the wording on the signs in the doorways (i.e., "bathroom #1," "bathroom #2," "bedroom #1," etc.) so that the contractors can provide the estimates for work on the correct rooms.

The pages that follow are examples of blank bid specification worksheets for homeowners to fill out with a description of the work that they want the contractors to give them prices for.

Figure 13-1 is an example of a blank bid specification worksheet for performing work on the exterior of the property.

Figure 13-2 is an example of a blank bid specification worksheet for a kitchen.

Figure 13-3 is an example of a blank bid specification worksheet for a bedroom.

Figure 13-4 is an example of a blank bid specification worksheet for a bathroom.

Figure 13-5 is an example of a blank bid specification worksheet for a living room.

Figure 13-6 is an example of a blank bid specification worksheet for a dining room.

Figure 13-7 is an example of a blank bid specification worksheet for a hallway.

Figure 13-8 is an example of a blank bid specification worksheet for plumbing, heating, electrical work.

Figure 13-9 is an example of a blank bid specification worksheet for miscellaneous work that was not covered under "room" or "exterior" categories (i.e., the removal of junk cars or other debris from the property).

<u>Bid Specification Worksheet (Blank)</u>

<u>EXTERIOR</u>	<u>PRICE</u>
ROOF:_____	$____
SIDING: _____	$____
LEADERS: _____	$____
GUTTERS: _____	$____
EXTERIOR PAINT: _____	$____
WINDOWS: _____	$____
YARD CLEANUP: _____	$____
FENCING: _____	$____
CEMENT WORK: _____	$____
SHUTTERS: _____	$____
STORMS/SCREENS: _____	$____
EXTERIOR DOORS: _____	$____
LANDSCAPING: _____	$____
LIGHTING: _____	$____
OTHER: _____	$____
OTHER: _____	$____
TOTAL:	$_____

Figure 13-1. Bid specification worksheet—exterior work.

Bid Specification Worksheet (Blank)

KITCHEN   **PRICE**

DIMENSIONS:

FLOORING: _____ $_____

PAINTING: _____ $_____

SPACKLING: _____ $_____

WINDOWS: _____ $_____

WALL COVERING: _____ $_____

DOORS: _____ $_____

STOVE/OVEN: _____ $_____

REFRIGERATOR: _____ $_____

OTHER APPLIANCES: _____ $_____

CABINETS:_____ $_____

COUNTERS: _____ $_____

PLUMBING:_____ $_____

ELECTRICAL: _____ $_____

LIGHTING FIXTURES: _____ $_____

OTHER:_____ $_____

OTHER: _____ $_____

     TOTAL: $_____

Figure 13-2.   Bid specification worksheet—kitchen.

<u>**Bid Specification Worksheet (Blank)**</u>

<u>**BEDROOM #1**</u>   <u>**PRICE**</u>

DIMENSIONS:

FLOORING: _____ $_____

WALL COVERING: _____ $_____

PAINTING: _____ $_____

SPACKLING: _____ $_____

CLOSETS: _____ $_____

ELECTRICAL: _____ $_____

HEATING: _____ $_____

WINDOWS: _____ $_____

ENTRY DOOR: _____ $_____

CLOSET DOOR: _____ $_____

LIGHTING FIXTURES: _____ $_____

OTHER: _____ $_____

OTHER: _____ $_____

OTHER: _____ $_____

OTHER: _____ $_____

OTHER: _____ $_____

   TOTAL: $_____

Figure 13-3. Bid specification worksheet—bedroom.

<u>Bid Specification Worksheet (Blank)</u>

<u>BATHROOM #1</u>   **<u>PRICE</u>**

DIMENSIONS:

FLOORING: _____ $_____

WALL COVERING: _____ $_____

PAINTING: _____ $_____

SPACKLING: _____ $_____

CLOSETS: _____ $_____

ELECTRICAL: _____ $_____

HEATING: _____ $_____

WINDOWS: _____ $_____

ENTRY DOOR: _____ $_____

CLOSET DOOR: _____ $_____

SINK: _____ $_____

LIGHTING FIXTURES: _____ $_____

TOILET: _____ $_____

SHOWER DOORS: _____ $_____

BATHTUB: _____ $_____

OTHER: _____ $_____

   TOTAL: $_____

Figure 13-4. Bid specification worksheet—bathroom.

<u>Bid Specification Worksheet (Blank)</u>

<u>LIVING ROOM</u>	<u>PRICE</u>
DIMENSIONS:	
FLOORING: _____	$_____
WALL COVERING: _____	$_____
PAINTING: _____	$_____
SPACKLING: _____	$_____
CLOSETS: _____	$_____
ELECTRICAL: _____	$_____
HEATING: _____	$_____
WINDOWS: _____	$_____
ENTRY DOOR: _____	$_____
CLOSET DOOR: _____	$_____
LIGHTING FIXTURES: _____	$_____
OTHER:_____	$_____
OTHER:_____	$_____
OTHER:_____	$_____
OTHER:_____	$_____
OTHER:_____	$_____
TOTAL:	$_____

Figure 13-5.   Bid specification worksheet—living room.

Bid Specification Worksheet (Blank)

DINING ROOM	PRICE

DIMENSIONS:

FLOORING: _____ $_____

WALL COVERING: _____ $_____

PAINTING: _____ $_____

SPACKLING: _____ $_____

CLOSETS: _____ $_____

ELECTRICAL: _____ $_____

HEATING: _____ $_____

WINDOWS: _____ $_____

ENTRY DOOR: _____ $_____

CLOSET DOOR: _____ $_____

LIGHTING FIXTURES: _____ $_____

OTHER: _____ $_____

OTHER: _____ $_____

OTHER: _____ $_____

OTHER: _____ $_____

OTHER: _____ $_____

   TOTAL: $_____

Figure 13-6. Bid specification worksheet—dining room.

Bid Specification Worksheet (Blank)

HALLWAY   **PRICE**

DIMENSIONS:

LOCATION:

FLOORING: _____ $_____

WALL COVERING: _____ $_____

PAINTING: _____ $_____

SPACKLING: _____ $_____

CLOSETS: _____ $_____

ELECTRICAL: _____ $_____

HEATING: _____ $_____

WINDOWS: _____ $_____

ENTRY DOOR: _____ $_____

CLOSET DOOR: _____ $_____

LIGHTING FIXTURES: _____ $_____

OTHER: _____ $_____

OTHER: _____ $_____

OTHER: _____ $_____

OTHER: _____ $_____

   TOTAL: $_____

Figure 13-7. Bid specification worksheet—hallway.

Bid Specification Worksheet (Blank)

TYPE OF WORK (PLEASE CHECK ONE)

( ) PLUMBING WORK

( ) HEATING WORK

( ) ELECTRICAL WORK

(Include Separate Worksheets for Each Category Listed Above)

PLEASE ITEMIZE BY ROOM, OR BY ENTIRE JOB:

	PRICE
_____	$_____
_____	$_____
_____	$_____
_____	$_____
_____	$_____
_____	$_____
_____	$_____
_____	$_____
_____	$_____
_____	$_____
_____	$_____
TOTAL:	$_____

Figure 13-8. Bid specification worksheet—plumbing/heating/electrical work.

Bid Specification Worksheet (Blank)

MISCELLANEOUS   **PRICE**

(PLEASE USE FOR WORK THAT DOES NOT FALL INTO OTHER ROOM CATEGORIES)

_____ $_____

_____ $_____

_____ $_____

_____ $_____

_____ $_____

_____ $_____

_____ $_____

_____ $_____

_____ $_____

_____ $_____

_____ $_____

_____ $_____

_____ $_____

_____ $_____

_____ $_____

TOTAL: $_____

Figure 13-9. Bid specification worksheet—miscellaneous.

Figure 13-10 is an example of a completed bid specification worksheet for work on the exterior of the house.

The homeowner fills out the bid specification worksheet with a description of the work he wants prices for, and each contractor is given a copy and asked to fill in the prices for the items listed.

The Notice to Bidders   Figure 13-11 is an example of a notice to bidders form, which, like the bid specification worksheet, can be customized for your particular needs. The following paragraphs explain the information that should be included in the form.

The contractor's name and contact information. This information helps you distinguish one contractor's estimate from another contractor's estimate.

The homeowners' names and contact numbers. This information helps the contractor to know how to reach you. It is also a good idea to indicate the best times to call.

Property address and directions. This information will help the contractor locate the correct property.

Access for entry to the premises. You have to arrange for the contractors to get inside and inspect the property so that they can prepare their estimates. The answers to the following questions will help you organize the manner in which the contractors are given access to the property. *If you are living in the house now:* Will you schedule appointments with each of the contractors to let them in, or will you delegate that task to someone else? *If the property is vacant:* Will you give the contractors a key and let them go there by themselves, or do you prefer to meet each of them there at different times that you can schedule in advance? *If the property is currently occupied by tenants:* You will have to set up appointments with the tenants for the contractors to have access.

Systems status. If possible, let the contractors know the present condition of the heating, ventilating, and air conditioning systems so that they can bring extra equipment with them, if necessary. For example, if the electrical system is not working, the contractors who are bidding on the job may need to bring a generator or some other energy source with them in order to test the systems and prepare their estimates for the work you want done. Any other systems with an electrical tie-in (such as an oil heating system) may also be affected.

Let the contractors know if there has been a recent fuel delivery, or if they will have to provide the fuel that they need to start up the system and test it. If you have purchased a foreclosure in a state with a cold climate in the winter months, and the heating system was winterized to prevent the pipes from freezing, the system has to be dewinterized so that, if necessary, the contractors can prepare their estimates to repair the heating system.

Bid Specification Worksheet

EXTERIOR   **PRICE**

ROOF: *Replace broken shingles where needed* _____ $_____

SIDING: *Paint white with brown trim (Need samples)* _____ $_____

LEADERS: *Install new leaders where needed* _____ $_____

GUTTERS: *Install new gutters where needed* _____ $_____

EXTERIOR PAINT: *See "siding" above* _____ $_____

WINDOWS: *Replace broken living room window* _____ $_____

YARD CLEANUP: _____ $_____

FENCING: *Remove left side* _____ $_____

CEMENT WORK: _____ $_____

SHUTTERS: *Paint to match brown trim* _____ $_____

STORMS/SCREENS: *Replace front entry storm door (Provide brochure)* ___ $_____

EXTERIOR DOORS: _____ $_____

LANDSCAPING: *Remove damaged tree from front lawn* _____ $_____

LIGHTING: _____ $_____

OTHER: _____ $_____

OTHER: _____ $_____

TOTAL: $_____

Figure 13-10.   Bid specification worksheet completed by owner—exterior.

NOTICE TO BIDDERS

CONTRACTOR'S NAME:_____ DATE:_____

HOMEOWNER'S NAME(S): _____

HOMEOWNER'S CONTACT NUMBER(S):

     NAME:_____ (___)_____

     NAME:_____ (___)_____

PROPERTY ADDRESS: _____

DIRECTIONS TO THE PROPERTY: _____

_____

_____

ACCESS FOR ENTRY: _____

SYSTEMS STATUS:

     Electric: On   Off   Date: _____

     Heating: Oil delivered   Not operating _____

     Winterized: Yes   No   Date: _____

ADDITIONAL INSTRUCTIONS: _____

_____

_____

DEADLINE FOR COMPLETING BID SHEETS: _____

(PLEASE NOTE: BIDS RECEIVED AFTER THIS DATE AND TIME ARE DISQUALIFIED).

Figure 13-11. A notice-to-bidders form.

Additional instructions. Let the contractors know your intentions for the use of the property. If you purchased it to rent out to tenants, you will most likely have different needs than if you are planning to live there with your family. For example, an investor who plans to rent the property to tenants will most likely prefer that the contractors install a commercial-quality carpeting to help make the premises as maintenance-free as possible. On the other hand, a property owner who will be moving into the house with his or her family may prefer a three-inch plush carpet.

You should make it clear that the specifications you have provided are by no means all-inclusive, and request the contractors to add any repairs that you may have missed (and the costs involved) directly to the bid sheet for that room.

If the work that the contractors perform will require a certificate of occupancy or similar documentation as evidence that the work was completed in compliance with the local building codes, this should also be noted so that the contractors can allow extra time for inspections by town officials when they calculate the length of time it will take them to complete the job.

Deadline for bidding. Let the contractors know the date that you would like to begin the work and the deadline for returning their completed bid sheets to you. Deadlines help prevent bid sheets from sitting in the glove compartment of the contractors' trucks.

The Bid Summary Sheet   The final document in the bid package is the *bid summary sheet.* After the contractors fill the bid specification worksheets, they use a bid summary sheet to list the final prices for each room as well as the total price for the job.

Each contractor must include the date that the job will be started and completed. If you intend to rent the property to tenants, the time it takes to complete the repairs is important. Depending on the extent of the work, you may not be able to have a tenant move into the premises until the work is complete, thereby eliminating your rental income. Thus, an investor who is waiting to rent out the premises may consider the completion date to be as important as the prices for repairs. The investor may even select a contractor that charges a couple of hundred dollars more than the other contractors because that contractor is able to complete the job a month earlier. (Under those circumstances, the extra couple of hundred dollars it will cost the investor is [more than] offset by [let's say] a $1500 monthly rental payment.)

On the other hand, if you are buying the foreclosure to live in, and the time of completion is not a material factor, you might select the contractor with the lowest prices—even when that contractor requires more time to complete the work than the other contractors.

Check to make sure that the contractor has included prices for all of the bid specification worksheets including the plumbing, heating, electrical systems, and the miscellaneous page (if applicable). It is also a good idea to check the contractor's totals for each room as well as for the total job. Figure 13-12 is an example of a bid summary sheet.

Setting Up a Comparative Cost Analysis Worksheet

After the contractors return their completed estimates, you can set up a worksheet that allows you to compare "apples to apples." Figure 13-13 is an example of a comparative cost analysis worksheet that you can use to compare and contrast the contractors' estimates.

Look for prices that are dramatically higher or lower than prices given by the other contractors. For example, if one contractor's price for the carpeting in bedroom #1 is a lot less than the prices given to you by the other contractors, the reason may be that the contractor will be installing an inferior carpet. On the other hand, the contractor with the low price may have a surplus of high-quality carpet left over from the last job that he or she completed and the savings are being passed on to you. To avoid problems of this nature, whenever possible, provide the contractors with samples of the carpet (and the padding) that you want installed. Also provide as much information as possible about the color, manufacturer, etc., to make it easier for the contractors to get prices.

If you do not have a particular product or color scheme in mind, you can request that the contractors provide you with samples of flooring material (carpet, padding, tiles, wood, linoleum), wall coverings (tile, wallpaper, paint, paneling), exterior siding materials (aluminum, vinyl, wood, shingles), roof shingles, and so forth, that they are basing their estimates on. Request samples of paint colors. (There are hundreds of shades of white.) Ask the contractors to provide you with brochures for appliances (i.e., are the prices based on rebuilt models rather than brand new ones?) plumbing and electrical fixtures, so that you can see the quality of the items the contractors are giving you prices for.

Awarding the Job

When you are satisfied that you have obtained prices for all of the work, select the contractor who can do the job within the time frame and budget that is most beneficial for you. Meet with the contractor, go over the bid results, and finalize the prices and completion date. The next step is to negotiate a payment plan that recognizes everyone's priorities.

BID SUMMARY SHEET

PROPERTY ADDRESS: _____

CONTRACTOR'S NAME: _____

CONTRACTOR'S ADDRESS: _____

CONTRACTOR'S TELEPHONE NUMBER: _____

_____

TOTAL PRICE OF JOB: $ _____

DATE WORK WILL BEGIN: _____

DATE OF COMPLETION: _____

ROOM/SYSTEM   **PRICE**

Exterior: _____ $____

Kitchen: _____ $____

Bedroom 1: _____ $____

Bedroom 2: _____ $____

Bedroom 3: _____ $____

Living Room: _____ $____

Dining Room: _____ $____

Bathroom 1: _____ $____

Bathroom 2: _____ $____

Hallway: _____ $____

Plumbing: _____ $____

Heating: _____ $____

Electric: _____ $____

   TOTAL JOB: $_____

Figure 13-12. A bid summary sheet.

		(1)	(2)	(3)	(4)	(5)	(6)	(7)	(8)	(9)	(10)
Job Total		Date Begin	Complete Date	Exterior	Bedrm #1	Bedrm #2	Bedrm #3	Living Room	Dining Room	Bath #1	etc.
	Contractor #1										
	Contractor #2										
	Contractor #3										
	Contractor #4										
	Contractor #5										

Figure 13-13. Comparative cost analysis worksheet.

Implementing a Performance-Based Payment Plan

Depending on the size of the job and the length of time it will take to complete, there are several options for paying a contractor. Some contractors prefer to be paid in three equal installments—one installment at the start of the job, one installment at the midpoint, and the final payment upon completion of the job. Other contractors prefer to receive half of the amount due when they start the job and the other half when they complete it. Unfortunately, problems can—and often do—arise when one party uses the system in a manner that harms the other party. One classic example is when the contractor gets paid up front, then disappears with the property owner's money (or goes out of business) and never returns to complete the work. This could cause a considerable amount of hardship for the homeowner, who may have given the contractor all of his or her savings, and cannot afford to pay someone else to complete the work. The only remedy available may be a lawsuit in the civil courts, which can take years to come to trial. And even if the homeowner is awarded a judgment against the contractor, it could be difficult to find any assets to seize, especially if the contractor has gone bankrupt or moved away without leaving a forwarding address. Many states have adopted contractor's licensing requirements to maintain high standards and eliminate fraudulent practices within the industry. Some states may also have established a fund that they use to help reimburse homeowners who were defrauded by dishonest contractors.

On the other side of the coin, the homeowner who is having the work done might not have enough money to pay the contractor after the work has been completed. Needless to say, this could be disastrous for the contractor who has already laid out a lot of money for labor and materials on that job, and needs to be reimbursed.

The payment policy that I have found to be most effective is where the contractor gets paid on a weekly basis for the work that was completed during the previous week. Here is how it works. Each week, on an agreed-upon day, the contractor calls the property owner with a list of the repairs that the contractor intends to complete by the end of the week. The property owner knows in advance the progress of the work and how much of a payment he will need to make at the end of the week. On the designated inspection day the property owner inspects the work that was performed and pays the contractor the price that the contractor assigned to it on the bid specification worksheet. For example, if the contractor gave the property owner a price of $250 for carpeting and $100 for painting in bedroom #1, and those items were inspected and confirmed to be complete, the property owner would pay the contractor $350.

The property owner benefits because a performance-based agreement inherently encourages expeditious results, and since the payment is only made after the work is completed, the owner is less vulnerable to a contractor's fraud. The contractor benefits because he or she does not have to wait long periods of time to be reimbursed for work that was completed, and can count on steady weekly paychecks.

The property owner and contractor must keep track of the payments made as the work progresses. In order to avoid accidentally paying for the same work more than once, both parties should keep copies of the checks paid to the contractor, and the dates and check numbers should be written in the margins next to each item on the bid sheet as that item is paid.

Establishing an Escrow Account

Another way that funds can be controlled is by setting up an escrow account. An escrow account ensures the contractor that the property owner has the funds available to pay him for his work.

The property owner deposits an amount of money into the escrow account that was contractually agreed at the time when the job was awarded to the contractor. An escrow agent (usually an attorney or a mediator) is selected and given specific instructions as to the conditions that must be met in order for funds to be released from the escrow account. The escrow agent is charged with releasing the funds to the contractor in accordance with those instructions.

Your attorney, accountant, and/or financial advisor should be contacted for assistance in setting up an escrow account and payment terms that will best suit your needs.

Developing the Contractor's Agreement

A well-defined contractor's agreement plays an essential role in helping property owners and contractors protect themselves when work is performed on a foreclosure.

As in any transaction, the agreement should be in writing, and its terms should meet the expectations of both parties. Any fee that you pay to have the agreement drawn up can save you thousands of dollars down the line because litigation is less likely to arise in situations where the terms of an agreement are clearly defined. The agreement should include the amount you have agreed to pay, the payment dates, and the terms you have agreed upon. Also of importance are the dates that the work will begin and end, and the default remedies in the event that the repairs are not completed in a timely manner. In states that require contractors to be licensed, the property owner should have a copy of the contractor's license that was issued by the state, and proof of insurance coverage. A copy of the final bid specification worksheet and the bid summary sheet with the start and completion dates should be attached as a rider to the agreement as well.

Figure 13-14 is a sample contractor's agreement. This agreement is just a sample of the terms and conditions that could be included. You should contact your attorney for more information about the state-specific terms and conditions that are applicable in your situation.

Other Contract Terms to Include

Penalties for late completion. The contract should stipulate the penalties that will be assessed against the contractor if the work is completed after the agreed-upon deadline. You may have chosen this contractor based on the earlier completion, even though the price was a little higher than the other contractors. If the job is unjustifiably delayed by the contractor, you should not be penalized by having to pay the premium price this contractor charged you, when you no longer have the benefit of the earlier completion date. If the contractor knows in advance that there will be stiff penalties assessed every day the job is delayed past the agreed deadline, that contractor will be more motivated to finish your job on time.

If you are an investor, you can base the penalty amount on the rental income you are losing because your tenant was unable to move in until the repairs were completed. For example, if your property has an expected monthly rental income of $900, you would set the penalty amount at $30 per day for each day past the agreed-upon deadline. On the other hand, if you live in the house (or will be living in the house after the repairs are complete) you can base the penalty on your mortgage payment, which is due to your lender every month whether you are living in the house or not. Accordingly, your daily penalty amount can be set at one-thirtieth of your monthly mortgage costs for every day the job is delayed past the agreed-upon deadline.

Rewards for early completion. A recent trend has emerged whereby contractors who were offered rewards for early completion of projects (such as widening of highways, repairing of bridges, etc.) completed the work early and received their rewards in a significant number of cases. Just as the threat of penalties is a powerful motivator, a reward for early completion has proven to be motivational as well. An early-completion reward is another option to consider as part of your agreement when the time frame for completion is of great importance.

PROPERTY OWNER AND CONTRACTOR AGREEMENT

This agreement is made this _____ day of _____ 20____ by and between _____, hereinafter called the homeowner and _____, hereinafter called the contractor.

For the consideration hereinafter named, the homeowner and the contractor agree as follows:

The Work: The contractor agrees to furnish all material and perform all work necessary to complete the repairs to the property located at: _____, in accordance with the specifications given by the homeowner and attached herewith.

The Time: The contractor agrees to promptly begin work as agreed to, and to complete the work as follows: Work to begin: _____ Date of completion: _____

A Penalty for work completed past the deadline will be assessed in the amount of $____ per day.

Extras: No deviation from the work or material specified in the specifications will be permitted or paid for unless a written work or change order is first agreed upon and signed as required.

Assignment: No assignment of this contract agreement is permitted without prior written permission from the homeowner.

Subcontractors: The contractor agrees to inform the homeowner about any subcontractors who will be hired by the contractor to perform on the job. The contractor agrees to provide the homeowner with any proofs of insurance or any other qualifications of any subcontractors who will be working on the job.

Insurance: The contractor agrees to obtain and pay for the following insurance coverage: worker's compensation, public liability, property damage, and any other insurance coverage that may be necessary or required by the homeowner or by state law.

Taxes: The contractor agrees to pay any and all federal, state, or local taxes that are, or may be, assessed upon the material and labor that are furnished under this contract.

Payment: The homeowner agrees to pay the contractor, for materials and work, the sum of $_____. A ____% retainage will be deducted from each payment to the contractor.

Payment terms, amounts, and dates, are agreed upon as follows: <u>ATTACH BID SPECIFICATIONS WITH FINAL PRICES AND BID SUMMARY SHEET.</u>

The homeowner and the contractor, for themselves, their successors, executors, administrators, and assignees, hereby agree to the full performance of the covenants herein contained.

DATE:_____   DATE:_____

_____   _____
Property Owner's Name   Contractor's Name

_____   _____
Property Owner's Signature   Contractor's Signature

Figure 13-14. A sample contractor's agreement.

Extensions of deadlines. Sometimes unforeseen disasters, such as hurricanes, tornadoes, or other weather conditions, cause delays that render the contractual deadline unrealistic. Additional work the property owner has requested that was not included in the original specifications could also cause work to extend past the deadline. A specific time limit should be agreed to whenever additional work is requested. If necessary, an extension should be granted (in writing). It is helpful to spell out in your agreement what you would consider acceptable as reasons for delays, and to incorporate the distinction between "reasonable" and "unreasonable" delays into your agreement. Figure 13-15 is an extension form for expanding the time frame to complete repairs without any penalties to the contractor. The form is not all-inclusive, and you should consult an attorney for state-specific terms that are applicable for your situation.

Waiver of mechanic's lien. Contractors working close to the financial edge may use the money you paid them for the work they performed on your foreclosure to pay for materials they purchased for a previous job. If the contractor does not pay off the debt, it is not impossible for the homeowner to find that a mechanic's lien was filed against his or her home. A mechanic's lien is a statutory financial claim against property, that is created in favor of contractors, laborers, and/or suppliers who have performed work or furnished materials to erect or repair a building and were not paid. I have heard horror stories from property owners who discovered liens filed against their homes by building supply companies, even though the property owners had paid the contractors in full for their jobs. You can help protect yourself by asking the contractor, as part of your contract terms, to provide you with a "waiver of mechanic's lien rights" for any subcontractors or material suppliers who provided labor or materials for your job. Contact your attorney for more information about protecting yourself from this heavy-duty headache.

Holding back a retainage. Another way that property owners protect themselves financially is to hold back a percent of the amount owed, called a "retainage," from each payment check. Thus, in the example given above where the contractor received payment in the amount of $350 for the painting and carpeting work completed in bedroom #1, you would hold back an agreed-upon retainage (I recommend 10 percent) from each payment made to the contractor. So, in this example, you would hold back $35, and the contractor would be paid $315. This may not seem like a lot of money now, but if the repair costs amount to thousands of dollars, the retainage you hold becomes much more significant. The retainage is usually released as the final payment to the contractor after all punch list items have been completed in accordance with the terms of the agreement between the contractor and the homeowner.

<u>Extension of Deadline to Complete Work</u>

DATE OF EXTENSION: _____

PROPERTY ADDRESS: _____

REASON FOR EXTENSION REQUEST: _____

ORIGINAL CONTRACT DEADLINE: _____

EXTENSION REQUESTED: _____

NEW CONTRACT DEADLINE: _____

AGREED TO:

(Date)_____   (Date)_____

_____   _____
Property Owner's Signature   Contractor's Signature

Figure 13-15. A sample contractor's extension form.

The final release of the retainage to the contractor can be contingent upon several things. For example, if the contractor is to provide you with a certificate of occupancy or its equivalent, then the retainage can be held back until the contractor provides you with that document. Retainage money can also be used by a property owner to hire a new contractor to complete a repair that the original contractor did incorrectly, or it can be applied toward damages stipulated in the contract if work is not completed in a timely manner. Retainage may also be held back from payments when you want to make certain that the plumbing, heating, or electrical systems that the contractor just finished working on continue to operate properly over a period of a few days. The percent of retainage that will be deducted from each check should be agreed to as part of the contract terms.

Frequency of inspections and payments for completed work. Be as specific as possible about the dates and times for inspections that will be performed in order for the contractor to be paid. The frequency of inspections and payments must be clearly defined, and so should the conditions that must be met for the retainage to be released by the property owner to the contractor.

The Big Picture

Whether you use all of these suggestions, some of them, or none, the most important thing is that the agreement you create meets the needs of each party. Ultimately, the best agreement is one where, at the end of its term, the homeowner and the contractor walk away with a great feeling that something wonderful was accomplished.

14

Getting Started
Today

Together we have looked at the benefits and risks involved with buying real estate foreclosures. The benefits are maximized and the risks are diminished when you put your time and effort into learning the foreclosure-purchasing procedure and then applying what you've learned towards fulfilling your dreams. In Chapter 14, we start you on your journey with six simple steps to help you turn your dreams into reality today.

Follow These Six Steps for Success in Purchasing Foreclosures

Step 1: Arrange Your Financing

If you will need financing in order to purchase your foreclosure, begin the procedure for getting your preapproval now. Your lending institution will let you know how much you can borrow based on your current income and credit rating. (See Chapter 9—*Questions to Ask a Lender When Shopping for a Preapproval.*)

If you have equity built up in the house you currently own and reside in, you can begin the procedure for obtaining an equity loan, a refinance, or a second mortgage to get the cash you need to buy your foreclosure. Chapter 6 helps you prepare a spreadsheet to use for comparing the financing terms that are offered by lending institutions. From there, you can select the loan with the best terms for your current needs and future goals. (See Chapter 6—*Figure 6.2.*)

Alternatively, if you know people who have the money to buy a foreclosure, but who have limited time to do the necessary legwork, think about purchasing with partners for now. You can offer your expertise as your contribution, or if you have some funds of your own available, you can contribute a portion of the funds to the transaction in return for a larger share of the equity stake in the property, as discussed in Chapter 8.

Another option to consider is an equity-sharing arrangement in which your role will be that of either the "insider" or the "investor." (See Chapter 8 for a complete discussion of this subject.)

Step 2: Develop Your Network of Support

You will need to find an attorney who is knowledgeable about foreclosure procedures to help answer your questions and protect your interests. Contact your local bar association and ask for a list of attorneys who specialize in real estate or foreclosure matters in your area. Ask the attorneys you contact for the fees they charge for their services before you hire them. Also ask for client referrals that you can contact for references. It is very important that you contact these clients to see if they were satisfied with the services the attorney provided. Is the attorney always accessible, or will you have to wait two weeks for your phone call to be returned? Was the attorney knowledgeable about all phases of the foreclosure-purchasing process? Does the attorney handle evictions? Because the fees and services provided by different attorneys will vary, I suggest that you contact several attorneys (and their client references) in order to develop a more accurate basis for comparison.

You will need an accountant or financial advisor who can review your specific financial situation and recommend the best monetary plan of action for you to pursue. Your friends or relatives may be able to recommend someone to you, and many certified public accountants and financial advisors advertise in the local telephone directory. Ask for information about the fees they charge for their services. Also, ask for references as you did when you were looking for an attorney.

You will need a reputable licensed contractor or engineer to assist you with your repair needs. Ask for references and photographs of work they have completed in the past. Contact your local consumer affairs office (or its equivalent) to confirm that the contractor or engineer is licensed with the appropriate government agency and to ensure that no complaints have been filed against the company or the individual.

You will need an insurance expert. Although the fees for some types of insurance are governed by state law, other types of insurance charges vary. With the assistance of an insurance expert, you can select insurance coverage that protects your interests at prices that fit your budget.

Step 3: Send for Your Foreclosure Lists

If you have decided to purchase your foreclosure at an auction, review Chapter 2 for the details concerning this opportunity, and send away for lists of upcoming auctions.

Chapter 3 is a great resource if you are interested in buying a bank-owned foreclosure after the auction. Begin by contacting lenders with

REOs in your area and asking them to send you lists of the properties in their inventories.

If you wish to pursue purchasing your foreclosure from a government agency, such as the DVA, HUD, GSA, or the FDIC, you can review the techniques in Chapter 4 for ordering lists of government-owned properties.

If you want to buy a foreclosure before the auction, the sources and strategies detailed in Chapter 5 can help you contact and negotiate with delinquent homeowners.

Step 4: Review Your Foreclosure Facts

Review the information contained in this book on a daily basis—until the procedures and the success that will result have become a part of you. Remember, *repetition is the mother of learning*. Review the checklists and the step-by-step activities, and then *picture your success in your mind*.

Step 5: Select the Property that Is Right for You and Do a Trial Run

Select the properties that are right for you, contact the appropriate parties, and ask the prebid questions (from Chapter 9) about the properties you are interested in. Inspect the premises and prepare your bid sheet as enumerated in Chapter 10. I suggest that you attend several auctions in order to experience the actual procedure in person, and to verify how you would have done if you *had* actually bid on the property. In so doing, you will build up your confidence as you learn to trust your own judgment. (Please note, however, that trial runs are *only* recommended *up to* the bidding point. Referees will get rather cranky if you call out a bogus offer because you forgot it was just a trial run and got caught up in the bidding!)

Step 6: Don't Give Up

No one has ever achieved success by quitting. Ben Franklin tried hundreds of times before he discovered electricity. Thank goodness he never gave up! (And he didn't even have a book like this to get him started!) To give you an idea of how crucial a role persistence plays in terms of success, under normal market conditions it takes approximately 4 times to contact a delinquent homeowner before you get a response. You will attempt to buy an REO 20 times before your offer for a bank or for a

<u>GETTING STARTED TODAY</u>

( ) **Step 1.** Arrange your financing.

( ) **Step 2.** Develop your network of support.

( ) **Step 3.** Review your foreclosure information daily until the procedure, and the success you will have becomes a part of you.

( ) **Step 4.** Send away for the lists of upcoming foreclosure sales.

( ) **Step 5.** Select the property that is right for you. Do a trial run.

( ) **Step 6.** Don't give up!

Not All-Inclusive—Additional Steps May Be Required

Figure 14-1.   "Getting started today" checklist.

government-owned foreclosure is accepted. You may end up preparing 25 bids and attending 25 auctions before you are the successful high bidder.

Remember: WINNERS NEVER QUIT...AND QUITTERS NEVER WIN!

A checklist titled "Getting Started Today" is provided as Figure 14-1. (It is not intended to be all-inclusive. Further steps may be necessary, as detailed throughout this book.)

From Rags to Riches with Real Estate Foreclosures

A foreclosure purchase is a great way to buy a property at a below-market price, keep it as a long-term residence or as an investment property rented out to others, or to "fix up" and "flip" for a large profit. Many real estate entrepreneurs have already acquired fortunes from this type of real estate transaction, and above all, I want to leave you with the knowledge and belief that you too can become successful. I hope I have given you the tools you need to *empower you with success **and** to help you achieve your goals.*

Index

Note: Boldface numbers indicate illustrations.

absolute auction, 15
access to properties, 119, 122, 143–151
adjustable rate mortgages (ARMs), 71, 75–77
after-auction foreclosure purchase, 11, 43–50, 43
after-closing checklist, **171**, 172
after-contract checklist, 163, **165**
alternative financing, 79–91
American Dream of Home Ownership, 96
amortized loans, 70
as-is condition, 22, 36
asking price, bank purchase of foreclosure and, 35
assignable contracts, 124
assumable mortgages, 74
at-auction foreclosure purchase, 11, 13–29
  as-is condition in, 22
  auction types and, 15
  bidding procedure in, 16
  delays in closing, unusual, 17–18
  dispossessing occupants in, 22
  finding upcoming auctions for, 25–28
  high bidder in, 17
  identification of property for, 16
  liens and, 23–25
  mortgage balance and less than market value
    price in, 21
  mortgage contingency clause in, 21
  multiple mortgages on one property and, 23–25
  newspaper announcements of auctions for,
    27–28, **28**
  no down payment refunds in, 21
  opening bid amount in, 16
  right of redemption by delinquent borrower in,
    22–23
  thirty-day close for, 17
  Torrens titles and, **17–21 19**
  traditional purchase vs., **25–28**
attorney's fees in mortgages, 72
auctions, 15
  absolute, 15
  bidding procedure in, 16
  bidding up a price, 16
  delays in closing, unusual, 17–18
  finding upcoming, 25–28
  high bidder in, 17, 155
  identification of property for, 16
  legal description of property, 16
  minimum bid, 15
  newspaper announcements of, 27–28, **28**
  opening bid amount or upset price in, 16
  thirty-day close for, 17
  verbal, 16
  with reservation, 15
  written, 17
awarding contractor's job, 192

balloon loans, 70
bank purchase of foreclosure (after auction), 29–42

bank purchase of foreclosure (*Cont.*):
  as-is condition in, 36
  asking price in, 35
  clear title in, 35
  defining bank-owned properties for, 31–32
  deposits or binders in, 40
  eviction of occupants in, 35
  finding REOs for, 36–38
  friendly foreclosure and, 32
  lender's view of bank-owned property and,
    problems with, 33–34
  lending institution advertisement of, 36
  "market value" defined for, 40
  negotiating strategies for, 40–42
  preparing your offer letter for, 38–40, **39**
  presenting your offer in, 35
  real estate office advertisement of, 38
  "real estate owned" (REO) and "owned real
    estate" (ORE), 32, 83
  REO purchase vs. bank auction, 35–36, **37**
  seller financing in, 35
  Web site advertisement of, 36, 38
  word of mouth/observation notice of
    foreclosures, 38
bankruptcy filing, 55, 61–62
before auction foreclosure purchase, 11, 51–62,
  83–84
beneficiary, in trust deeds, 9
bid calculation worksheet, **145**
bid sheets, 141–151
  condition of property and occupancy status,
    143–151
  final confirmation in, 151
  limits to bids and, 148
  prior-to-bidding checklist for, **150**
  worksheet for, **145**
bid summary sheet for contractors, 191–192, **193**
bidding, 5
bidding up a price, 16
binders, 40
boarded-up houses, 122–123
broom clean, 22
bulk purchase of foreclosures, 90–91
buyout option defaults, for partnerships and equity
  sharing, 108
buyout terms, for partnerships and equity sharing,
  107

call out of bids, 16–17
carrying charges, monthly, 104–105
cash flow, 138–140, **139**
  in income-producing properties, 98
  partnerships and equity sharing, 102
cash purchases, 90
causes of delinquency in payment, 53
certificate of occupancy, 126, **127**, 134–135
challenges of partnership owners, 96

choosing right property, 115–140, 207
clear title, 35
closing costs, 100, 103–104
closing dates, 123
closing day, 40, 157–159, 169
   bank purchase of foreclosure and, 40
   delays in closing, unusual, 17–18
   30-day period to, 17
closing documents, 169
community services (*See* utilities on premises)
comparative cost analysis worksheet for contractors and repair work, 192, **194**
comparison shopping for best lender rates, 71–72, **72**
competitive bidding by contractors, 176–194
complaint, mortgage and, 8
condition of property, 67, 143–151
confidentiality, waiver of, 57
contacting delinquent owners, 58–61, **60**
contract terms, 61, 102–103, **103**
contract transfers, 84–85, **85**
contractor/investor, in partnerships and equity sharing, 109, 111–112, **111**
contractor's agreement, 196–197, **198**
contractors and repair work, 175
   awarding the job for, 192
   bid specifications worksheets for, 177–194, **179–187**
   bid summary sheet for, 191–192, **193**
   comparative cost analysis worksheet for, 192, **194**
   competitive bid package for, 176–194
   competitive bidding by contractors for, 176–194
   contractor's agreement in, 196–197, **198**
   contractors for, 175
   credit of contractors for, 177
   deadline for bidding on, 191
   escrow accounts for, 196
   extending deadlines for, 199, **200**
   inspections and, 201
   instruction sheets for bidders in, 191
   notice to bidders for, 188, **190**
   penalties for late completion in, 197
   performance-based payment plan for, 195–196
   prioritizing, 175
   retainage hold-back in, 199, 201
   rewards for early completion in, 197
   subcontractors and, 177
   waiver of mechanic's liens and, 199
court order, in Torrens title, 20
credit limits and mortgages, 75
credit ratings, 41, 54

damage to property, 33
deed in lieu of foreclosure, 32
deed, **18**
deeds of trust (*See also* trust deeds), 5–8, **6**
default provisions, 3
default, **4**
deficiency judgment, 32
delayed financing, 91
delinquent homeowner/borrower, 3
   bankruptcy filing by, 55, 61–62
   contacting, 58–61, **60**
   credit rating of, 54
   equity saving for, 54
   future income saving and, 54
   hard money loans for, 55
   in lieu of foreclosure deed and, 56
   negotiating with, property has equity, 55–56
   negotiating with, property with negative equity (short sales), 56–57

delinquent homeowner/borrower (*Cont.*):
   payment plans for, 56
   preventing worse trouble for, 54–55
   waiver of confidentiality and, 57
   bid accepted by, 156–157
   helping, 54–55
   understanding motivation of, 53
Department of Housing and Urban Development (HUD), 46, **47**, 83
deposits, 40
depreciation deduction, in partnerships and equity sharing, 106
dispossessing occupants, 22
disputes, in partnerships and equity sharing, 108
down payment, 98, 100, 123
   in partnerships and equity sharing, 102, 103–104, 103
   no refund on, 21
dressing for success, when dealing with delinquent owners, 59
"dumping" of foreclosures, 34

earnings, in partnerships and equity sharing, 100, 102
employment qualifications for mortgages, 73
engineer's report, **136**
equity financing, 81–83, **82**
equity sharing (*See also* partnerships), 93–113
equity splitting, in partnerships and equity sharing, 106
escrow accounts
   for contractors and repair work, 196
   for mortgages, 74–75, 74
eviction costs, 135
eviction of occupants, 35, 170
extending deadlines for contractors and repair work, 199, **200**

Fannie Mae (Federal National Mortgage Association) sales, 49
Federal Deposit Insurance Corporation (FDIC) sales, 48
Federal Home Loan Mortgage Corporation (Freddie Mac) sales in, 49
Federal Housing Authority (FHA) loans, 46, 68, 70, 68
Federal National Mortgage Association (Fannie Mae), 49, 73
financing, 205
finding partners for equity sharing, 112–113
finding upcoming auctions, 25–28
first mortgagee, 23
fixed-rate mortgages, 67–68, **69**
foreclosure notices, inspection of, 131
foreclosure search, 8
foreclosures
   legal procedure of, overview of, 3–5
   understanding, 1–12
Freddie Mac (Federal Home Loan Mortgage Corporation) sales, 49
friendly foreclosure, 32

getting started, 203–209
goals of partnerships and equity sharing, 113
goals of property ownership, 96–97
Government Services Administration (GSA) sales, 45–46
government-backed mortgages, 67
government-owned property, 45–49, 83, 156, 159
   Department of Housing and Urban Development (HUD) and, 46, **47**

government-owned property (*Cont.*):
  Federal Deposit Insurance Corporation (FDIC) sales in, 48
  Federal Home Loan Mortgage Corporation (Freddie Mac) sales in, 49
  Federal National Mortgage Association (Fannie Mae) sales, 49
  FHA foreclosures and, 46
  Government Services Administration (GSA) sales and, 45–46
  invitation for bids (IFB) in, 46
  Veterans Administration (VA) sales, 48
graduated-payment mortgages (GPMs), 71
greetings letter for occupants, 160–161, **162**, 163, **164**

hard money loans, 84
  delinquent owners and, 55–56
helping delinquent owners, 54–55
hidden costs, 133
high bidder at auction, 17, 155
holds paper, holds mortgage, 70
Home Loan Guaranty Services Web page, 48
homeowner's insurance, 105, 133–134, 157
HomeSteps Foreclosure Listing, 49

in lieu of foreclosure deed, 56
income producing properties, 96–97, 163
income tax benefits, for partnerships and equity sharing, 105–106
indexes for mortgages, 75
inside investor and outside partner, 95
inside occupant, 101
inspecting a property, 119–121
  contractors and repair work, 201
instruction sheets for bidders, 191
insurance coverage, homeowner's and life, 105, 133–134, 157
insurance policies, borrowing against, 85–86
interest (*See also* mortgage interest deduction), 106
interest rates, 73–74, 97–98, 100, 102
interest-only mortgage payments, 70
investor/contractor, in partnerships and equity sharing, 109, 111–112, **111**
invitation for bids (IFB), government-owned property and, 46

jumbo loans, 73

last-owner search, 24
late charges, 3
leases, execution of, 172
legal description of property, 16
legal notices of foreclosures, 58
lender's margin in mortgages, 75–76
lending institution advertisement of foreclosures, 36
length or term of mortgage in, 66–67, **69**
liabilities to bank, 33
liens or judgments, 23–25, 126
life cap, in ARMs, 76
life insurance coverage, 105
liquidated damages, 21
lis pendens, mortgage, 8–9, 58

market value, 21, 107, 137–138
  bank purchase of foreclosure and, 40
  partnerships and equity sharing, 107
mechanic's liens, waiver of, 199
memorials, in Torrens title, 20
minimum bid auction, 15
missing property documents, 134
monthly carrying charges in, 104–105

monthly mortgage payments, in partnerships and equity sharing, 100–101
mortgage balance, 21
mortgage contingency clause, 21
mortgages, 5–8, **7**, 63–77, 159, 205
  adjustable rate (ARMs), 71, 75–77
  amortized loans and, 70
  assumable, 74
  attorney's fees in, 72
  balloon loans, 70
  comparison shopping for best lender rates, 71–72, **72**
  complaint on, 8
  condition of property and, 67
  conventional vs. government-backed, 67
  credit limits and, 75
  decisions affecting, 65–67
  employment qualifications for, 73
  escrow accounts for, 74
  Federal Housing Authority (FHA), 68, 70
  Federal National Mortgage Association (Fannie Mae), 73
  filing of foreclosure papers on, 8–9
  fixed-rate, 67–68, **69**
  foreclosure on, 8–9
  foreclosure search on, 8
graduated-payment (GPMs), 71
  indexes for, 75
  interest rates and, locking in, 73–74
  interest-only payments (*See also* balloon loans), 70
  lender's margin in, 75–76
  length or term of mortgage in, 66–67, **69**
  life cap in, 76
  lis pendens on, 8
  negative amortization in, 76–77
  origination fee in, 74
  owner-occupant status in, 66
  points in, 74
  prepayment penalties in, 74
  questions to ask lender about, 72–77
  seasoning before loan approval and, 75
  security for, burden of proof in, 65
  summons on, 8
  term cap in, 76
  terms of sale on, 9
  time line of ownership and, 66
  Veterans Administration (VA) loans, 68, 70
mortgage interest deduction, 106
mortgage, lien, and judgment search, 24

moving occupants, 163
multiple mortgages on one property, 23

negative amortization in mortgages, 76–77
negative cash flow, in income-producing properties, 98, 102
negotiating
  bank purchase of foreclosure and, 40–42
  delinquent owners and, property has equity, 55–56
  delinquent owners and, property with negative equity (short sales), 56–57
neighbors to watch property, 158
network of support, 206
newspaper announcements of auctions/foreclosures, 27–28, **28**, 58
nonperforming assets of bank, 33
note and mortgage (*See also* mortgages), 5–8, **7**, 73
notice of pending action, 58
notice to bidders for contractors and repair work, 188, **190**

notices of foreclosure, 206–207
notifying occupants, 160–161, **162**, 163, **164**

occupancy status, 124–125, 126, **127**, 143–151
  notifying occupants, 160–161, **162**, 163, **164**
offer letter, for bank purchase of foreclosure,
  38–40, **39**
opening bid amount, 16
operating expenses, in partnerships and equity
  sharing, 106
origination fee in mortgages, 74
outside investor, 102
outside partner, 95
overhead expense to banks, 33
owned real estate (ORE), bank purchase of foreclosure and, 32, 83
Owner's Duplicate Certificate of Title (ODC) (*See
  also* Torrens title), 17–21, **19**
owner-occupant status, mortgages and, 66
owner-occupant vs. partnerships, 98, **99**, 100

parents and children, partnerships and equity
  sharing, 109, **110**
partnerships and equity sharing, 86–87, **88, 89,**
  93–113
payment defaults, in partnerships and equity
  sharing, 108
payment plans, delinquent owners and, 56
penalties for late completion, contractors and
  repair work, 197
performance-based payment plan, contractors and
  repair work, 195–196
permits, rental properties, 129, 135, 160
points in mortgages, 74
power-of-sale clause, trust deeds and, 9
pre-auction foreclosures, finding, 57–58
prequalified loans, 117–119, 159, 205
preapproved loans, 117–119, 159
prebid questions, **132**
preliminary property inspection, 119–121
prepayment penalties in mortgages, 74
prepossession of property, 125
presenting your offer, in bank purchase of
  foreclosure, 35
prevention against future borrowing in partnerships and equity sharing, 107–108
price of property, 117
prior-to-bidding checklist, **150**
Property Disposal Web page, 46
property taxes, 135–136
protecting the property, 124, 157–158, 161
public notice, 5
purchase price limits, in partnerships and equity
  sharing, 103
purchasing foreclosures, 10–11
  after the auction, 11, 29, 43–50
  at the auction, 11, 13–29
  before the auction, 11, 51–62

questions to ask lender about mortgages, 72–77

real estate office advertisement of foreclosures, 38,
  58
"real estate owned" (REO), bank purchase of
  foreclosure and, 32, 83
referees, 5, 17
refinancing a mortgage, 81–83, **82**
rent collection, 97
rental permits, 129, 135, 160
rental properties (*See* income-producing properties)

repairs and other expenses (*See also* contractors
  and repair work), 105, 124, 135, 147, 149,
  169, 173–201
repurchase by original owner, 163
reservation auctions, 15
restrictive zoning, 129–130
retainage hold-back, contractors and repair work,
  199, 201
rewards for early completion in contractors and
  repair work, 197
right of redemption by delinquent borrower,
  22–23, 125–126
risks, partnerships and equity sharing, 108

safety tips for inspections, 120–121
sealed written offers, 17
search, foreclosure, 8
seasoning before loan approval, 75
second mortgage, 23, 81–83, **82**
seller financing, bank purchase of foreclosure and,
  35
selling the property, 160
short sales, 56–57
Soldier's and Sailors Civil Relief Act of 1940, 10
specifications worksheets, 177–194, **179–187, 189**
subcontractors, contractors and repair work, 177
summons, mortgage and, 8
support network, 206
surveys, 126, **128**, 134

tax issues, 105–106, 135–136, 170, 172
tenant problems, 97
term cap in ARMs, 76
term of mortgage, 66–67, **69**
terms of sale, 9, 131–132
30-day close, 17
time line of ownership and mortgages, 66
title insurance, 158–159
title search, 24, 131, 158–159
Torrens title, 17–21, **19**, 123–124
traditional purchase vs. buying at auction, 25–28,
  26
trust deeds, 5–8, **6**
  foreclosure on, 9–10
  power-of-sale clause in, 9
  trustor, trustee, and beneficiary in, 9
trustee, in trust deeds, 9
trustor, in trust deeds, 9

U.S. Real Estate Property Sales List, 46
understanding delinquent owners, 53
upset price, 9, 16
utilities on premises, 122, 130–131, 135, 169–170

value of property, establishing, 137–138
verbal bidding auctions, 16
Veterans Administration (VA) loans, 48, 68, 70, 68

waiver of confidentiality, 57
waiver of mechanic's liens and, 199
Web site advertisement of foreclosures, 36, 38
winterizing property, 33, 122
with reservation auction, 15
word of mouth/observation notice of foreclosures,
  38
written auctions, 17

yodeling, of auctioneer, 16

zoning restrictions, 129–130